Transference and Empathy in Asian American Psychotherapy

Transference and Empathy in Asian American Psychotherapy

CULTURAL VALUES AND TREATMENT NEEDS

Jean Lau Chin, Joan Huser Liem,
MaryAnna Domokos-Cheng Ham,
and
George K. Hong

PRAEGER

Westport, Connecticut
London

Library of Congress Cataloging-in-Publication Data

Transference and empathy in Asian American psychotherapy : cultural
   values and treatment needs / Jean Lau Chin . . . [et al.].
         p.   cm.
   Includes bibliographical references and index.
   ISBN 0-275-94493-X (alk. paper)
   1. Asian Americans—Mental health. 2. Psychotherapy. 3. Asian
Americans—Psychology. 4. Psychotherapist and patient.
5. Psychiatry, Transcultural—Case studies.   I. Chin, Jean Lau.
   [DNLM: 1. Asian Americans—psychology. 2. Cultural
Characteristics. 3. Empathy. 4. Physician-Patient Relations.
5. Psychotherapy. 6. Transference (Psychology)   WM 420 T7717]
RC451.5.A75T73   1993
616.89′14′08995073—dc20
DNLM/DLC
for Library of Congress   92–48757

British Library Cataloguing in Publication Data is available.

Library of Congress Catalog Card Number: 92-48757
ISBN: 0–275–94493–X

First published in 1993

Praeger Publishers, 88 Post Road West, Westport, CT 06881
An imprint of Greenwood Publishing Group, Inc.

Printed in the United States of America

∞™

The paper used in this book complies with the
Permanent Paper Standard issued by the National
Information Standards Organization (Z39.48–1984).

10 9 8 7 6 5 4 3 2 1

Contents

Part II Case Discussions

Part III Conclusion

Preface

During the last decade there has been increased recognition of the need for clinical training programs and curricula directed at preparing therapists to work more effectively with ethnic minority clients in general and, more specifically, with Asian American clients (Shon, 1979; Wong, 1986). Bernal and Padilla (1982) note the dearth of curricula in training programs nationwide that address the needs of low-income and ethnic minority populations. Wong (1986) describes the state of the art in mental health service delivery to Asian American communities and calls for an increase in culturally sensitive training and curricula.

In August 1987, the Department of Mental Health and Social Service of the South Cove Community Health Center, Boston, and the Psychology Department of the University of Massachusetts–Boston, Harbor Campus, cosponsored a two-day interactive forum on transference and empathy in psychotherapy with Asian Americans. The issues of transference and empathy were chosen as the foci of the forum because they address two critical aspects of the therapeutic relationship that the conference organizers believed need to be reexamined in the context of Asian American cultural values and treatment needs. The specific goals of the forum were:

- To bring together a critical mass of Asian American mental health professionals and agencies nationwide to examine issues critical to psychotherapy with Asian American populations.

- To support Asian American practitioners in documenting their clinical experiences with Asian Americans.

- To develop training materials for the education of mental health professionals providing psychotherapy to Asian American populations.

- To develop a partnership between the academic community and community agencies.

- To develop an interactive-forum format to serve as a model for training.

- To enhance theory development and clinical practice relevant to Asian Americans.

Both theoretical papers and clinical case presentations were commissioned for the interactive forum.

This book evolved from and incorporates major issues discussed at the forum. Part I summarizes the main concepts of the theoretical papers. In the chapters on transference and empathy, Jean Chin and MaryAnna Ham have also included their own conceptualizations of these two critical aspects of the therapeutic relationship. Part II contains, in their entirety, the cases to provide clinical material to illustrate psychotherapeutic processes and concepts and a focus for discussions of theory and practice. In all of the case studies the names and certain identifying data have been altered or withheld to ensure confidentiality. The case authors, who all conduct psychotherapy using the client's primary language, bring to their cases their unique orientations, and these chapters illustrate the importance of cultural and linguistic variables in influencing the therapeutic process. In the cases included in this book, Gloria Chieko Saito conducted her psychotherapy using English and a psychodynamic approach; George Hong conducted his psychotherapy using Cantonese Chinese and a cognitive behavioral approach; Siu Ping

Ma conducted her work using Cantonese Chinese and an eclectic approach combining systems, psychodynamic, and psychosocial approaches; and Jennie Yee conducted her work using English and an eclectic approach. In Part III, Joan Liem links theory and practice.

Questions and exercises have been included at the end of each chapter to stimulate discussion and the exploration of specific issues related to transference and empathy. The questions, which in Parts I and II are specific to the chapters, are designed to provoke thought and to raise issues rather than to bring closure, since it is our sense that these issues are relevant to the emergence of different perspectives on the practice of psychotherapy for Asian American and other ethnic minority clients.

This volume is intended to be used as a training manual for mental health providers of Asian American clients. We hope it will become part of the training curricula of academic institutions committed to training culturally sensitive clinicians and of agencies providing clinical service to ethnic minority clients. We also hope it will serve to further the development of theory regarding psychotherapy with ethnic minority clients.

REFERENCES

Bernal, M. E & Padilla, A. M. (1982). Status of minority curricula and training in clinical psychology. *American Psychologist*, 37(7), 780–787

Shon, S. P. (1979, May). The delivery of mental health services to Asian Americans. In *Civil rights issues of Asian and Pacific Americans: Myths and realities. A consultation sponsored by the U.S. Commission on Civil Rights* (pp. 724–733) (GPO:1980 624-865/1772). Washington, DC: U.S. Government Printing Office.

Wong, H. Z. (1986). Mental health services in Asian and Pacific American communities: Directions for training programs and curricula. In *Practice in minority communities: Development of culturally sensitive training programs* (pp. 177–198). Washington, DC: U.S. Dept. of Health and Human Services, National Institute of Mental Health.

Acknowledgments

We would like to acknowledge the following presenters and participants in the Interactive Forum on Transference and Empathy in Psychotherapy with Asian Americans held in Boston in August 1987: Christine Chang, M.D.; Weining C. Chang, Ph.D.; Peter Kim, M.D., Ph.D.; Siu Ping Ma, M.S.W.; Gloria Chieko Saito, Ph.D.; Chong Suh, Ph.D.; Herbert Wong, Ph.D.; David Wu, Ph.D.; Joe Yamamoto, M.D.; and Jennie H. Y. Yee, Ph.D. A special thanks to Deborah Sussewell Brome, Ph.D., for her participation and assistance in planning and organizing the forum.

We would also like to acknowledge the support provided by a Joseph P. Healey Grant from the University of Massachusetts at Boston, which made the conference possible. The forum was cosponsored by the Psychology Department of the University of Massachusetts at Boston and by South Cove Community Health Center, Boston.

We would like to give special thanks to David McGill, Psy.D., for his close reading and thoughtful comments on an earlier draft of this manuscript. We appreciate the careful attention Timothy Moynihan gave to the preparation of the annotated bibliography. We would also like to thank Michael Macmillan for editing the manuscript and Christine Keung and Phyllis Doucette for their assistance in preparing it.

Part I

Theoretical Issues

Contextual Factors in Psychotherapy with Asian Americans

George K. Hong

Before discussing transference and empathy, it is essential to have an overview of how Asian Americans differ from other ethnic and racial groups in the ways they conceptualize mental health and illness. This influences their use of mental health services and their expectations of psychotherapy. Asian American is used here as a general term to include diverse people from different countries in Asia. It is impossible to discuss every individual Asian country or ethnic group. However, because of their proximity to one another and because of the historical interaction among them, Asian countries, especially those in the Pacific area, share many cultural features. Historically, Chinese culture was a major influence on the cultures of other countries in the area. In addition, Confucianism, Buddhism, and Taoism strongly influenced the cultures of China, Japan, Korea, and other Asian countries. Such philosophical orientations distinguish East Asian people from those of Western countries, American as well as European, which are dominated by a Judeo-Christian heritage. In this regard, it is possible to speak of Asian Americans as a group in contrast to the majority of the American population, which is of European heritage. Instead of examining every aspect of Asian cultures, I will focus on the major characteristics of Asian Americans that are especially relevant to the provision of mental health services.

Asian Americans are currently the fastest growing minority group in the United States. Their numbers have more than doubled from 3.5 million in the 1980 census to 7.3 million in the 1990 census. Their current numbers represent 2.9 percent of the U.S. population; by the year 2000, their numbers could total 9.9 million or 4 percent (Gardner, Robey, & Smith, 1985).

In spite of the dramatic increase in numbers, Asian Americans remain the third largest racial or ethnic minority, trailing sharply behind African Americans (30 million or 12.1% of the total U.S. population) and Hispanic Americans (22.4 million or 9% of the total U.S. population), according to the 1990 census. As such, Asian Americans are a minority among minorities and are often neglected when minority issues in mental health are examined.

The findings of Sue and McKinney (1975), Wong (1982), and Yamamoto (1978) indicate that Asian American clients often drop out of treatment prematurely and often seek psychotherapy only upon experiencing acute breakdown or severe psychopathology. Sue (1977), Kim (1978), and others argue that low service utilization among Asian Americans reflects not a lack of need but rather a lack of responsiveness by practitioners to the special needs of Asian American clients. Differences between Asian Americans and other client groups as well as differences among Asian Americans, such as their county of origin, immigration history, number of generations in the United States, and degree of English facility, must be taken into account for effective therapeutic intervention.

Cultural variables often define help-seeking behaviors, symptom manifestation, and attitudes toward the therapeutic process. Although many clinicians are beginning to recognize the need for therapeutic approaches that are more responsive to the cultural values and needs of Asian Americans, little exists in the literature on how to accomplish this task (Chin, 1980). This book addresses this need by focusing on two critical aspects of the therapeutic relationship: transference and empathy. Transference and empathy are widely acknowledged in the mental health literature as central to psychotherapy. By examining how they need to be conceptualized differently with Asian American clients, this book will help clinicians achieve a better understanding of psychotherapy with this population and adapt their therapeutic techniques accordingly.

CULTURAL PERCEPTION OF PSYCHOTHERAPY

Asian Americans often perceive and approach psychotherapy differently from other Americans. Most Asian Americans are totally unfamiliar with the practice of psychotherapy (Gaw, 1982; Hong, 1988; Lee, 1979, 1982; Shon & Ja, 1982; Sue & Morishima, 1982). When a person develops a serious mental disorder, family members often expect the clinician to treat the problem like a physical ailment. Since they conceptualize their problems somatically, they tend to find traditional Western psychotherapeutic practices difficult to understand. They expect medication and immediate relief of symptoms and are confused by the process of "talk therapy." They also tend to see mental health providers as doctors who treat "crazy" people. Consulting such a doctor is perceived as stigmatizing and is therefore largely avoided when a client is experiencing a minor emotional problem or stress from a life situation. If a client does not experience serious symptoms, he or she will probably not seek psychotherapy. Many Asian languages do not even have words to describe psychological disorders as Western cultures characterize them. Hence, a therapist often has to engage a client by educating him or her about the nature of psychological problems and the process of psychotherapy.

An Asian American client's reluctance to see mental health services is further reinforced by the emphasis within Asian cultures on the family as the major support system (Hong, 1988, 1989; Lee, 1982; Shon, 1979; Shon & Ja, 1982; Sue & Morishima, 1982; Wong, 1985). In contrast to Western cultures, which focus on the individual, Asian cultures focus on the family. Family members are expected to help one another when there is a problem. This expectation radiates from the nuclear family to the extended family, and in some cases to the entire village or community. The family expects to contain and resolve problems within itself. Asking for outside help is perceived as exposing the family's problem to others and revealing the family's inadequacy. As such, it brings shame upon the family. Furthermore, mental illness is considered an embarrassment that needs to be kept confidential and within the family. Whether a client is going to a therapist to address a major life transition or a serious mental disorder, the cultural prohibition again discussing personal or family issues with outsiders (i.e., the therapist) will be a major hurdle to overcome. This is especially true because psychotherapy typically involves discussion of intimate personal and family issues. Thus, many Asian Americans see psychotherapy only as a last resort, after existing resources within the family support system have been exhausted (Gaw, 1982; Hong, 1988; Lee 1979, 1982; Lorenzo & Adler, 1984; Shon & Ja, 1982; Sue & Morishima, 1982; Wong, 1985). When Asian Americans do seek psychotherapy, therefore, therapists must be sensitive to the hesitation and inhibition their clients may experience. Rather than interpreting such hesitation as evasiveness or defensiveness, therapists have to familiarize themselves with and accept their clients' cultural definition of the situation. They must help their clients examine and understand the very real tension between family loyalties and personal distress.

Asian Americans are often referred for mental health services by medical professionals because they tend to experience their emotional problems psychophysiologically. Even when it is not a matter of somatization, clients still find it easier to approach non-mental health professionals such as medical doctors or teachers who already have an established helping relationship with them. Since these professionals are familiar and respected authority figures in Asian cultures, they are frequently consulted. In contrast, the mental health profession does not exist in traditional Asian cultures. It is a product of Westernization. In many Asian countries, mental health services are still limited to the medical practice of psychiatry. Many people simply do not know when it is appropriate to consult a therapist for psychotherapy. Indeed, the question of how mental health professionals should present themselves and how they should relate to the Asian American client is central to the discussion of transference and empathy that follows.

Since many Asian Americans are unfamiliar with mental health services, they have the same expectation for therapy as they have for other helping professions. When they consult a medical doctor, they obtain medication and directions for health care. When they ask a teacher or an authority figure about a life situation, they receive advice and directions. When they accept a referral for psychotherapy, they also expect to obtain some direct instructions from the mental health provider. Therapy is assumed to be focused on problem solving, not talking about feelings and emotions. Clients some in with specific questions or problems and expect the therapist to provide answers and advice (Hong, 1988, 1989; Lee, 1982; Lorenzo & Adler, 1984; Shon & Ja, 1982; Sue & Morishima, 1982). Regardless of their theoretical orientations, therapists must be prepared to respond adequately to this expectation. Otherwise it is unlikely that the client will return for a second session. The clinical cases in Part II of this manual illustrate how different therapists have addressed this issue.

CULTURAL FACTORS WITHIN THE THERAPY SESSION

During a psychotherapy session, there are also cultural factors that need to be considered. One issue is that Asian Americans often differ from other ethnic and racial groups in their styles of communication. Indirect and nonverbal expression is a common style of communication in Asian cultures (Hong, 1989; Shon & Ja, 1982). Western modes of psychotherapy emphasize direct and open expression of thoughts and feelings. Direct confrontation with authority figures or the expression of strong negative feelings to strangers is often avoided in order to be "polite." Thus, a therapist has to be sensitive to nonverbal communication such as tone of voice and body language in order to comprehend fully how the client is feeling or what the client is really saying.

Another issue is that a therapist has to be careful about what is considered by the culture as too intrusive for discussion in the early stages of a relationship. For example, detailed family background, family income, and sexual relationships are often considered too personal to be discussed in an initial session unless there is an obvious association with the presenting problem (Hong, 1989; Lee 1982). By understanding and respecting these cultural norms, the therapist is in a better position to engage the Asian American client.

ENVIRONMENTAL AND SOCIAL ISSUES

There are also environmental and social issues that therapists have to be informed about when working with Asian Americans. Asian American immigrant groups often face problems beyond their personal emotional problems. Sometimes, these problems are so serious that they are presenting problems *and* the focus of treatment. At other times, they are simply background psychosocial stressors that therapists must be aware of when addressing the presenting problem.

Stressors of Recent Immigrants

New immigrants often experience stress and barriers in adjusting to a new lifestyle and culture in the United States (Hong, 1989; Lee, 1982; Shon & Ja, 1982). Many of those from lower socioeconomic-status groups lack facility in English or appropriate job skills to seek employment in mainstream settings. They have to compete for the limited jobs within ethnic settings; many get stuck in low-paying jobs with little opportunity to move ahead socially or financially. For some refugee groups, war trauma and the trauma of migration compound the difficulties inherent in making the transition to American society.

Regardless of socioeconomic status, many new immigrants also face the loss of the traditional family support system they relied on in their country of origin. In times of need, they find themselves depending upon public service agencies that are difficult to access and often not culturally sensitive or knowledgeable enough to serve them adequately. These agencies are often not equipped to serve non-English-speaking clients. These are all issues that a therapist working with the Asian American population has to address.

Second-Generation Concerns

Asian Americans who have been in the United States longer, especially maturing adolescents or U.S.-born children of immigrant parents, often experience problems that are different from those encountered by new immigrants. A prominent example is the development of cultural identity (Hong, 1989; Lee, 1982; Lorenzo & Adler, 1984; Sue, 1973; Sue & Morishima, 1982). At one time or another, many Asian Americans face the question of clarifying who they are: "Are they Asian or are they American?" As two of the clinical cases in this book illustrate, such identity issues can be serious enough to be a focus of therapy. For children who have become more Americanized than their parents, the cultural gap may also result in family conflicts. Differences between American culture and Asian cultures abound; they range from routines of daily living to social and family expectations. Issues of parental authority, definitions of independence, and expectations about responsibility to the family that grow out of contrasting Asian and Western values are often sources of friction between family members. Differences between parents and children in their familiarity with English and their native language limits communication.

Even those Asian Americans who have been in the United States for many generations have to deal with problems associated with their minority status. They may still find themselves the targets of racial discrimination, either blatant or subtle, just because they have Asian physical features or because of their presumed affiliation with their countries of origin. The internment of Japanese Americans during World War II is a cogent example. Barriers to employment and career advancement faced by ethnic minorities in this country are prominent examples that affect every Asian American group.

The environmental, social, cultural, and identity issues just discussed are further compounded for children of Asian Americans who have intermarried with other racial or ethnic groups. As one of the clinical cases in this book demonstrates, the confusion, pain, and stress experienced by such an individual can be serious and may require long-term therapeutic intervention.

The issues discussed in this overview are ones that a therapist working with the mainstream population does not have to confront. They highlight the need to train culturally knowledgeable and sensitive clinicians to serve Asian Americans. But this is just an overview of the most frequently encountered issues. We cannot provide here a comprehensive discourse on Asian American mental health, but rather we direct the reader to the references cited in this chapter for more detailed information on these issues.

The following chapters deal with transference and empathy, which are critical aspects of the therapeutic relationship central to psychotherapy, and examine their implication in working with Asian Americans. These discussions are followed by four case presentations that examine how transference and empathy, as well as the above cultural, social, environmental, and identity issues, manifest themselves and are addressed in psychotherapy with Asian American clients.

DISCUSSION QUESTIONS

1. How many Asian American groups can you identify? What cultural elements do they share? How are they different from each other?

2. Which are the major Asian American groups in your state or area? What are the particular historical, social, and environmental factors of which one must be aware in providing psychological services to each of them?

3. Which differences among Asian American groups are based on immigrant generation (foreign born, first generation American, second generation, etc.) and which on ethnic origin?

4. To what extent does ethnic identity impact on the psychological development of a person? Is this impact different among first, second, and third generation Asian Americans?

5. What does it mean to be a culturally competent therapist? What does it take for one to be culturally competent in providing psychological services to Asian Americans?

6. Pick a specific Asian cultural value. How might this value influence how an Asian American client presents himself or herself in psychotherapy?

7. How might minority status, immigrant status, or socioeconomic status influence perceptions and utilization of psychotherapy?

8. Pick an Asian philosophical orientation. State its five major tenets. How are these tenets different from or similar to the major tenets of psychotherapy? What implications does this have for psychotherapy practice with Asian Americans?

REFERENCES

Chin, J. L. (1980). *Mental health for Asian Americans in the 80s: Diagnosis and psychotherapy considerations.* Paper presented at the Conference on Mental Health in the 80s at the Smith College School of Social Work, Northampton, MA.

Gardner, R. W., Robey, B., & Smith, P. C. (1985). Asian Americans: Growth, change, and diversity. *Population Bulletin, 40*(4), 1– 43. Washington, DC: Population Reference Bureau.

Gaw, A. (Ed.) (1982). *Cross-cultural psychiatry.* Boston, MA: John Wright–PSG.

Hong, G. K. (1988). A general family practitioner approach for Asian American mental health services. *Professional Psychology: Research & Practice, 19(6),* 600–605.

——— (1989). Application of cultural and environmental issues in family therapy with immigrant Chinese Americans. *Journal of Strategic and Systemic Therapies* [Special issue], *8* (Summer), 4–21.

Kim, B.L.C. (1978). *The Asian Americans: Changing Patterns, changing needs.* Urbana IL: Association of Korean Christian Scholars in North America.

Lee, E. (1979). Mental health services for the Asian Americans: Problems and alternatives. In *Civil rights issues of Asian and Pacific*

Americans: Myths and realities. A consultation sponsored by the U.S. Commission on Civil Rights (pp. 734–756 (GPO: 1980 624-865/1772). Washington, DC: U.S Government Printing Office.

————— (1982). A social systems approach to assessment and treatment for Chinese American families. In M. McGoldrick, J. K. Pearce, & J. Giordano (Eds.), *Ethnicity and family therapy* (pp. 527–551). New York: The Guilford Press.

Lorenzo, M. K. & Adler, D. A. (1984). Mental health services for Chinese in a community health center. In *Social Casework, 65*(10), 600–609.

Shon, S. P. (1979). The delivery of mental health services to Asian Americans. In *Civil rights issues of Asian and Pacific Americans: Myths and realities. A consultation sponsored by the U.S. Commission on Civil Rights* (pp. 724–733) (GPO: 1980 624-865/1772). Washington, DC: U.S. Government Printing Office.

Shon, S. P., & Ja, D. Y. (1982). Asian families. In M. McGoldrick, J. K. Pearce, & J. Giordano (Eds.), *Ethnicity and family therapy* (pp. 208–228). New York: The Guilford Press.

Sue, D. W. (1973). Ethnic identity: The impact of two cultures on the psychological development of Asians in America. In S. Sue & N. N. Wagner (Eds.) *Asian-Americans: Psychological perspectives.* Palo Alto, CA: Science and Behavior Books.

Sue. S. (1977). Community mental health services to minority groups: Some optimism, some pessimism. *American Psychologist, 32(8)*, 616–624.

Sue, S., & McKinney, H. (1975). Asian Americans in the community mental health care system. *American Journal of Orthopsychiatry, 45*(1), 111–118.

Sue, S., & Morishima, J. K. (1982). *The mental health of Asian Americans.* San Francisco: Jossey-Bass.

Wong, H. Z. (1982). Mental health services in Asian and Pacific American communities. In L. R. Snowden (Ed.), *Reaching the underserved: Mental health needs of neglected populations. Annual review of community mental health.* Newbury Park, CA: Sage.

————— (1985). Training for mental health service providers to Southeast Asian refugees: Models, strategies, and curricula. In T. C. Owan (Ed.), *Southeast Asian mental health: Treatment, preven-*

tion, services, and research (pp. 345–390) (DHHS Publication No. ADM 85-1399). Washington, DC: National Institute of Mental Health.

Yamamoto, J. (1978). Therapy for Asian Americans. *Journal of National Medical Association, 70,* 267–270.

Transference

Jean Lau Chin

While clinicians approach psychotherapy from a variety of theoretical perspectives, they share a definition of psychotherapy first
and foremost as an interpersonal process. As therapists attempt to
achieve therapeutic outcomes, they must first engage clients in a
therapeutic relationship. This therapeutic relationship is a precon-
dition for change in psychotherapy. It is differentiated to include
both the real and the projected aspects of therapist characteristics
(Greenson & Wexler, 1969; Langs, 1978). The real aspects often
form the basis for a therapeutic alliance. The projected aspects
often reflect past relationships with a parent or significant other
that are played out in the context of the client-therapist relationship, that is, transference.

The concept of transference originates in and has been central
to psychodynamic theory. Transference refers to a client's reactions to the therapist as they are determined by fantasy and unconscious factors. Viewing the therapist in terms of past relationships
leads to irrational attitudes, feelings, and distortions (Dewald,
1971; Giovacchini, 1972; Greenson, 1965; Langs, 1974, 1978). In
identifying the transference process, the therapist provides the
client with an opportunity to examine feelings about the prior

relationship and to work through conflicts and maladaptive behavior patterns. A close examination of this transference process corrects the ill effects of previous relationships and becomes the basis for change in psychotherapy.

Classical psychodynamic theory emphasized the neurotic transference derived from relationships with one's parents and was based on the triangulation inherent in the oedipal relationship (Greenson, 1965). More recently, object relations theory has emphasized the self as key to the transference relationship. Psychotherapy is viewed as correcting failures in the development of the self. As a result, narcissistic transference and restoration of the self have become more central to change in the psychotherapeutic relationship (Kohut, 1971). These self-object transferences sustain the cohesion, vitality, or organizing capacity of the self. Consequently, "transference should be understood as a much broader process encompassing the repetition of established information-processing patterns directed toward maintaining the function of the self system and/or expanding its influence" (Basch, 1986, p. 28).

CULTURE AND THE PSYCHOTHERAPEUTIC RELATIONSHIP: IMPORTANCE FOR ASIAN AMERICAN CLIENTS

While the concept of transference has been central to psychodynamic theory, the influence of culture on these aspects of the therapeutic relationship has generally been given little attention. Although it has become increasingly clear that race, class, and culture are significant variables in the practice of psychotherapy (Acosta, Yamamoto, & Evans, 1982; Chin, 1981; Dudley & Rawlins, 1985; Gardner, 1980; McGoldrick, Pearce & Giordano, 1982; D. W. Sue, 1978; S. Sue, 1982; Thomas & Sillen, 1972; Yamamoto, James, & Palley, 1968), the emphasis is often on sensitivity to differences in cultural content. It is generally recommended that therapists learn about the cultural values and practices of the client in order to be sensitive in their therapeutic practice.

As a result, we know little about how culture influences the quality of the psychotherapeutic relationship. We understand even less well how transference becomes manifest in the psychotherapeutic relationship between a therapist and an Asian American client. Some authors have questioned the usefulness of a psychodynamic model with Asian American populations (Toupin, 1980), suggesting that the emphasis on the ideal client (i.e., young, attractive, verbal, intelligent, and single) favored white, middle-class clients and precluded clients from different cultural backgrounds. Viewing Asian culture broadly, one might argue that, given the cultural value placed on regulation of emotions rather than their release, Asian American clients would be less prone to catharsis. One might also argue that they would be less verbally productive given the cultural value placed on brevity.

Chin (1987) calls attention to the fact that psychotherapy relies on prescribed rules of practice that are, in fact, rooted in a cultural context. Although most therapists are sensitive in "educating" clients to the rules prescribed for the therapeutic context (e.g., 50-minute session, confidentiality), most take for granted the prescribed rules of conduct for the interpersonal context. This occurs primarily because culture normally provides the common, but unspoken, context to facilitate communication and interpersonal behavior. However, the contrast between Western and Asian cultures often results in miscommunication that only serves to increase the distortions projected by the client onto the therapist in the transference. Therefore, it is critical to understand how cultural differences may influence the transference relationship with Asian American clients and how transference phenomena might differ in psychotherapy with Asian Americans.

CULTURAL MANIFESTATIONS IN THE THERAPEUTIC ALLIANCE

Before we can understand how culture becomes manifest in the projected aspects of the therapeutic relationship, that is, the transference relationship, it is important to understand how culture becomes manifest in the real aspects of the therapeutic relationship, that is, the therapeutic alliance. As contextual variables, cultural values and worldviews influence the interpersonal aspect of the therapeutic relationship. Because Asian cultures subscribe to the Confucian view of filial piety, which values unquestioning obedience to parents and those in authority positions (Tseng, 1973), Asian clients in psychotherapy often are more deferent in the therapeutic relationship. The emphasis and value placed on subordination and mutual dependence in the therapeutic relationship are often greater than for Western clients. Asian clients also expect the therapeutic relationship to be hierarchical in contrast to the Western emphasis on assertiveness and equality. In psychotherapy, these discrepancies could be problematic if the therapist expects the client to take responsibility while the client expects the therapist to be an authority figure and to give advice. Educating the client about the "rules" of introspection, catharsis, or free association intrinsic to psychodynamic psychotherapy is often ineffective if cultural values reinforce listening and ego regulation as criteria for self-actualization. An effective therapeutic alliance is developed only if the relationship is reframed to fit with the worldview and cultural values of the Asian client, a point that is illustrated by the clinical cases presented in this volume.

Weining Chang (1987) has reviewed the cognitive and language dimensions of the therapeutic alliance and has stressed their importance to the therapeutic relationship with Asian American clients. The ability to conduct therapy in the primary language of the client rather than through translators often has a profound effect on the therapeutic alliance. De La Cancela (1985) describes how language switching can be used by bilingual clients in psychotherapy to express different emotional experiences. Culturally specific communication patterns are also apparent in the therapeutic relationship. Western values often stress getting one's point across, whereas Asian values stress politeness in verbal discourse. As a result, Westerners are likely to value verbal fluency, whereas Asians are likely to value not interrupting others. Therapists who fail to understand this different style of interpersonal communication are likely to face barriers in establishing a therapeutic alliance. Subtle linguistic nuances also convey significant semantic differences in the therapeutic relationship. Metaphors are commonly used by clients to communicate specific affective states or experiences; since these metaphors are often language-specific, translations may lose the significance of the client's intent.

Nonverbal communication such as body language, spatial boundaries, facial expressions, eye contact, and touching also have different connotations in different cultures (Hall, 1976). Asian cultures, for example, have been defined as high-context cultures where individuals rely more heavily on the nonverbal context for information than on the verbal context. Consequently, the therapeutic alliance will be enhanced with Asian American clients if greater attention is paid to nonverbal, contextual communication. Silence, for example, cannot be interpreted as agreement if the client is being polite in not contradicting the therapist.

Whereas the "real" aspects of the therapeutic relationship are subject to distortions due to different cultural interpretations, the "projected" aspects of the therapeutic relationship will be distorted yet further. These distortions can be influenced by cultural worldviews, which Derald W. Sue (1978) defines as how a person perceives his or her relationship to the world, and therefore the psychotherapeutic relationship. Ibrahim (1985) stresses the importance of organizing human experience in the context of individual worldviews to enhance effectiveness in cross-cultural psychotherapy. Asian worldviews, therefore, influence concepts of fate, time, and causality, which, in turn, influence the choices Asians make in adapting to their environments. For example, maturity is viewed as having established an interdependence within the family network in contrast to a Western emphasis on independence. The regulation of emotions is deemed more important to ego development in Asian cultures than the release of emotions advocated in Western cultures. Asian cultures also emphasize harmony with one's environment in contrast with Western emphasis on mastery of one's environment. How these differences influence the transference relationship will be described next.

CULTURAL MANIFESTATIONS IN THE TRANSFERENCE RELATIONSHIP

Only recently has the literature begun to suggest that race and sociocultural factors play a significant role in the transference relationship (Greenson, Toney, Lim, & Romero, 1982; Zaphiropoulos, 1982). Zaphiropoulos (1982) suggests that psychoanalysis has ignored the dimension of culture in its theoretical conceptualizations. The initial emphasis on a developmental approach, dynamic constellations, and specific defenses suggested a universal approach to establishing the psychotherapeutic relationship. This presented a barrier to viewing transference phenomena as culturally specific.

In working with Asian American clients, differences in culture and race create a context that is different from what is "normal" and expectable in the client-therapist relationship. Comas-Diaz and Minrath (1985) point out that the introduction of race and culture into the therapeutic relationship will catalyze transference themes of self-image, race, social class, identity, and anger. Often, these themes cannot be separated from projections related to the psychodynamic issues of the client. Consequently, we must determine how and if "classic" conceptualizations of neurotic and mirror transferences, for example, need to be altered or refined when working with an Asian American client. Several transference themes common among Asian American clients are described below.

Hierarchical Transference: Authority

For all clients, perceptions and feelings about the therapist are influenced by the authority status of the therapist. Given the importance of hierarchical relationships in Asian culture, Asian American clients will attribute greater value to the authority status of the therapist. The concept of hierarchical transference defines this phenomenon. Transference reactions with Asian American clients will more commonly emphasize notions of filial piety and respect for authority, By defining the therapeutic relationship in hierarchical terms, Asian clients will more often view the therapist as an all-knowing advice giver or as a wise and caring authority figure whose recommendations are to be followed. Because the authority figure is idealized in Asian culture as a benevolent figure, hierarchical transference is likely to be positive in tone and associated with compliance rather than rebellion.

Whether hierarchical transference facilitates or hinders depends on individual dynamics and how therapists are likely to use the transference. As the clinical cases presented in this volume suggest, Asian American clients with domineering and intrusive parents are likely to experience this as negative and will benefit from therapeutic analysis of the hierarchical transference. Clients with authoritative but supportive parents are likely to experience this transference as positive and facilitative of the therapeutic alliance. The presence of a hierarchical transference can also be facilitative in evoking higher expectations of cure and better compliance. Use of authoritative directives rather than reflective interventions can be more facilitative with a hierarchical transference. However, it can also inhibit spontaneity and delay open communication in the early phases of psychotherapy. This delay has often been misconstrued as communication failure in psychotherapy with Asian American clients.

The issue of accepting and working with a hierarchical transference versus transcending the hierarchical transference was a central focus of the Interactive Forum on Transference and Empathy in Psychotherapy with Asian Americans held in Boston in 1987. While participants agreed that a hierarchical transference tends to occur more frequently with Asian American clients, some participants argued that a hierarchical transference is inevitable and that it is important to utilize it to facilitate change in psychotherapy. Chong Suh (1987), on the other hand, advocated transcending the hierarchical relationship in psychotherapy with Asian Americans. She believed the therapist needed to provide a corrective experience to effect change.

Several variables may influence the emergence of a hierarchical transference: the gender of the client-therapist dyad and the degree of acculturation of both client and therapist may be two crucial variables. It is likely that a female therapist is more able to transcend the hierarchical relationship because her professional role is likely to supersede and be dystonic with her social role. A male therapist, on the other hand, is more likely to be confined by the hierarchical transference because his professional role is syntonic with his social role. Male clients are also more likely to be tied to traditional hierarchical roles, whereas females are more motivated to transcend these traditional roles, given the traditionally inferior status of women. For females, transcending the hierarchical transference relationship is empowering and, therefore, likely to be facilitative in psychotherapy. For males, transcending the hierarchical transference is likely to elicit greater conflict because it forces them to give up idealized notions of superior male roles and authority status in Asian culture.

Racial Transference: Power

Race in American society has been associated with issues of power, social status, and discrimination. As a result, race is generally an important aspect of identity for ethnic minority individuals. Given this emphasis, racial awareness is heightened whenever there is a non-white individual in the client-therapist dyad. Both therapists and clients are more likely to make attributions related to ethnic minority status and race. Consequently, transference feelings related to racial background are more likely to arise in the therapeutic relationship if either or both members of the client-therapist dyad are ethnic minority individuals. The concept of racial transference characterizes those attitudes toward the therapist related to race that have no basis in the therapeutic context. However, in contrast to other transference reactions, racial transference generally cannot be separated from reality-based reactions related to race. Asian clients are likely to make attributions about the therapist's race not only as a result of personal life circumstances, but also as a result of the sociocultural context associated with race relations in the United States.

The power differential in the therapeutic relationship is crucial to the concept of racial transference. When an Asian client is able to view the therapist as a benevolent authority figure and positively identifiy with the therapist, he or she will be more able to benefit from this inequality of status and power. When an Asian client is struggling with feelings of racial inferiority, several reactions are common. With a white therapist, the client may react with anger and hostility in response to past experiences and expectations of discrimination. On the other hand, the client may identify with the aggressor and become overly compliant and self-effacing. White therapists are often blinded by their own stereotypes about Asians. With an Asian therapist, an Asian client who is struggling with feelings of inferiority may experience the therapist as incompetent and lacking in authority.

Ethnic minority clients often will experience powerlessness and helplessness in response to the different race of the therapist. This racial transference can be facilitative for clients with strong ethnic/self identities whereas it may be a hindrance for clients who are ambivalent about their ethnic/self-identity. Racial transference reactions are often heightened with lower-class minority clients whose experience of powerlessness is associated with economic disadvantage. Empowerment, or the experience of control over one's destiny, becomes an important therapeutic outcome when a racial transference is present. This can be achieved only by supporting a positive identification with the client's race and in working through the racial transference. Asian clients struggling with issues of inferiority may pay the price of experiencing inferiority with their own race if not matched with a therapist of the same race; on the other hand, they may be unable to establish a therapeutic alliance with a therapist of their own race.

Self-Object Transference: Ethnic/Self-Identity

In line with emergent object relations theory, self-object transferences sustain the cohesion, vitality, or organizing capacity of the self. Whereas ethnic identity is intricately related to self-identity for Asian clients, as it is for most ethnic minority individuals, transference reactions with Asian American clients will also reflect crucial aspects of ethnic identity. Wong (1987) emphasized that the racial/ethnic identity of the therapist may contribute to feelings of admiration or affirmation of inferiority status in the transference. During the interactive forum, he spoke of myths and stereotypes as precursors to transference phenomena and emphasized the importance of drawing from the history of an ethnic group to understand the manifestation of self-identity in the transference.

In recognizing the importance of ethnicity in the definition of self-identity with Asian American clients, we must reconceptualize existing notions of self-object transferences described in the literature by Kohut (1971). Self-object refers to a dimension of experiencing an object in which a specific bond is required for maintaining, restoring, or consolidating the organization of self-experience. These self-object dimensions may serve mirroring, idealizing functions and lend cohesion, continuity, and positive affective experience to the self-experience (Stolorow, 1986). Therefore, self-object transferences for Asian clients will often include a prominent ethnic dimension. Thus, it is important to validate, maintain, or restore a client's ethnic identity in the therapeutic relationship. Sometimes this can be done only with a same-race match in the client-therapist dyad to provide a positive ethnic role model for self-identification. This is often more crucial when reality-based racial or cultural issues or conflict over ethnic identity are heightened. Sometimes this is done when the therapist is able to mirror an adaptive resolution of self-identity together with ethnic identity.

The concept of a bicultural identity as opposed to acculturation into the Western world is important when working with self-object transferences. For Asian clients, integrating Asian and Western cultural values and practices is often a challenge at best. Conflicts about ethnic identity are a major part of the normal developmental process. To achieve this process, self-experiences may need to be viewed in discontinuous terms; lack of consolidation may be essential because cultural values are incompatible. In developing a bicultural identity, Asian clients may utilize sophisticated split-ting mechanisms, although this is generally viewed as a primitive defense mechanism. Unless we acknowledge these differences in the process of developing a self-identity for Asians and other ethnic minority clients, we have but a partial understanding of self-object traansferences when working with Asian American clients.

Preoedipal Transference: Ethnic Gender Roles

As women's roles in society evolved following the women's liberation movement, related changes were also seen in the practice of psychotherapy. Psychodynamic theory has been reconceptual-ized in light of feminist thinking. Gornick (1986) and Gilligan (1982) have both called attention to the manner in which the inequality of female roles in society has been recapitulated in psychodynamic models. The Oedipus complex, which emphasizes male development and the paternal-child bond, is a prime example. Erotic or neurotic transferences, reflective of unresolved oedipal issues, were once viewed as central to psychodynamic psychother-apy. Preoedipal transferences, based on the maternal-child bond, were viewed as more pathological and developmentally primitive.

Understanding Asian development and culture demonstrates how ethnocentric this was. Yamamoto and Chang (1987) describe the Ajase complex as more syntonic with the Asian culture than the Oedipus complex:

> In contrast to the Oedipus complex, Japanese psychoanalysts have focused upon the Ajase complex, which is based on a myth: Prince Ajase not only kills his father, as does Oedipus, but he has a very special and culturally syntonic relationship with his mother. The Indian myth of Prince Ajase reflects the intense Japanese mother-son relationship. Prince Ajase, who was destined to kill his father, becomes king. He later tries to kill his mother because she is loyal to his father, the dead king. However, Ajase is not able to accom-plish this because of his guilt feelings. Apparently, as punishment for his transgressions, sores develop on his body, and an odor emanates from them so offensive that no one will come near. His

mother is the only person willing to care for him. King Ajase's heart responds to this mother's display of affection and forgiveness, thus he and his mother are reunited. (Okonogi as quoted by Tatara, 1980, cited by Yamamoto, 1987, p. 21)

Unlike Oedipus from the Greek tradition, Ajase from the Buddhist tradition emphasizes the mother-son dyad rather than the father-son dyad. In Ajase, the guilt feelings are raised because of the mother's love for her son, whereas in Oedipus, the guilt feelings are due to the fear of retaliation by the father (Iwasaki, 1971).

These issues suggest the need to reconceptualize preoedipal or narcissistic transferences that render dominant feminine themes less equal and more primitive than male ones. Benedek (1973) and Mogul (1982) have observed that women therapists are more likely to trigger both primitive wishes for reunion with the preoedipal mother and fears of either engulfment or abandonment by the mother. The oedipal or erotic transference of traditional psychodynamic theory essentially validates a Western male perspective. Freud's (1915) writing on the erotic transference assumes more or less explicitly that the patient is a woman and that the analyst is a man.

Although male dominance has been fairly universal in most cultures, each culture evolved different cultural practices to sustain this social hierarchy. In working with Asian clients, the dominance of mother-son themes within the culture suggested by the Ajase complex will mean that preoedipal transferences will be more prominent. However, preoedipal transferences will need to be conceptualized along a different, but equally complex, developmental continuum. The prominence of guilt, somatization, and unconditional maternal love will influence the nature of the pre-oedipal transference.

As late arrivals to the United States from cultures vastly different from "mainstream" America, Asian Americans have also been slower to challenge a male dominant social hierarchy. Historically, Asian cultures were also highly stratified along social class, gender, and authority lines. Women were expected to defer to men in social, academic, and familial relationships. Classic Chinese folklore romanticized women who disguised themselves as men to enter occupations open only to men (i.e., military, scholar). Chinese opera often used male actors for female roles. This historical sociocultural context undoubtedly influences feminine gender roles and their manifestation in the transference relationship.

Four types of transferences have been described to illustrate how cultural and racial differences influence the nature of the psychotherapeutic relationship. Hierarchical and racial transferences add a new dimension to the status differential in the psychotherapeutic relationship that has been largely ignored in the discussion of transference. These perspectives, which are different from "classical" psychodynamic theory, illustrate the need to reconceptualize concepts of self-object and preoedipal transferences. In working with Asian American clients, transference phenomena are related to gender, culture, and identity; therapeutic interventions need to reflect the different values and worldviews of the client.

CULTURAL BIAS AND COUNTERTRANSFERENCE

Transference phenomena among Asian American clients cannot be fully understood without recognizing the cultural distortions brought to the psychotherapeutic relationship by the therapist. These distortions influence the countertransference phenomena of the therapist and can include the theoretical frameworks and cultural perspective of the therapist. Although cultural sensitivity is emphasized in working with ethnic minority populations, emphasis is often placed on therapists learning about a client's culture. Just as Asian clients will develop transference reactions related to gender, culture, and identity, therapists working with Asian clients will also develop countertransference phenomena related to these same issues.

First, the theoretical framework used by a therapist in psychotherapy will reflect the countertransference phenomena of the therapist. Cultural values of the therapist can influence the therapist's opinion about the treatability of a client, what is average and expectable in the therapeutic relationship, and development phenomena. These "cultural countertransferences" can easily blind therapists, causing them to interpret culturally different behavior as examples of resistance or noncompliance. For example, modesty among Asian clients has been viewed as a hindrance to free association in psychodynamic psychotherapy. This perspective views cultural differences as negative phenomena to be overcome in psychotherapy. Positive reframing of these cultural phenomena would result in greater cultural sensitivity. In applying this perspective to transference phenomena with Asian American clients, emphasis would be on how an Asian client's modesty can be used to facilitate the therapeutic process. Emphasis would also be placed on different types of transference (e.g., hierarchical) manifested by an Asian client rather than failures of certain transference phenomena to appear (e.g., oedipal). Finally, emphasis would be on reconceptualizing "classical" transference phenomena (e.g., self-object) in a way that is culturally relevant.

The cultural perspective of the therapist also shapes countertransference manifestations. Psychotherapy with Asian American clients often poses the dilemma of educating the client in the ways of Western psychotherapy versus molding psychotherapeutic practice to the ethos of the client's culture. Therapists who view psychotherapy as involving a set of "standard" practices will experience difficulty in working with Asian American clients. This perspective suggests that effective psychotherapy is possible only if deviations from or modifications of this "standard" practice are made. Therapists who can view psychotherapy as but another culture will more easily establish a therapeutic alliance with an Asian client necessary for psychotherapy to proceed. Wu (1987) argues for the importance of cultural empathy, which empowers the client as a partner in the therapeutic process. He challenges therapists to attempt to understand the meaning from the client's cultural perspective and not assume that clinical phenomena identified in standard theoretical frameworks are universal. Reframing psychotherapy from this anthropological perspective helps to view transference phenomena as different rather than as deviant.

Asian American therapists seeing Asian American clients will potentially experience yet different forms of countertransference phenomena. Sharing a similar cultural heritage often facilitates the development of a positive transference. However, Asian American therapists can also be prone to overidentify with and overprotect an Asian American client. This can occur through underdiagnosing and normalizing maladaptive forms of behavior. Asian American therapists working with Asian American clients may also have difficulty transcending culturally prescribed roles. With strong taboos against divorce, it may be more difficult, for example, to appropriately confront an Asian client about his or her failed marriage.

CONCLUSION

Little has been written about the therapeutic alliance, transference, or countertransference in the psychotherapeutic relationship with Asian American clients. This chapter identifies some differences in the transference phenomena presented by Asian American clients because of their culture and their ethnic minority status. Therapists working with Asian clients need to recognize the interaction of transference and cultural phenomena. It is important that the psychotherapy literature incorporate these different perspectives in order to advance the development of effective psychotherapy with Asian American clients.

DISCUSSION QUESTIONS

1. How does a client's culture influence the nature of the transference relationship?

2. Are there types of transference relationships that are more prominent with Asian American clients? Is a "hierarchical transference" more characteristic of the therapeutic relationship with an Asian American client?

3. For which clients is a hierarchical transference facilitative and when? For which clients does it hinder psychotherapy and when?

4. What does it mean to transcend a hierarchical transference when one is working with an Asian American client whose culture defines many relationships in hierarchical terms?

5. When is it therapeutically important to transcend the racial/ethnic transference? How can it be achieved?

6. Will attributions and feelings about the racial/cultural background of the therapist manifest themselves more frequently in therapeutic relationships with Asian American clients than with white clients? What implications does this have for technique? Are there differences in the ways in which attributions and feelings about the therapist are manifested among other ethnic minority groups as well?

7. Considering the issue of pretransference and the role of racial/ethnic identities in the development of a therapeutic alliance, what steps should be taken by a therapist who is non-Asian American to facilitate a positive transference with an Asian American client, especially at the initial stage of therapy? For the Asian American therapist, does being of the same racial/ethnic background as the client create any difficulties and pitfalls? What precautions should be taken?

8. How do gender issues influence the transference relationship with Asian American clients? Will the influence be modified by the race/ethnicity of the therapist? Are such influences similar or different for clients of other ethnic minority groups?

9. How do the ages of therapists and clients influence the transference relationship with Asian American clients?

10. Based on your experience in working with Asian American clients, are there other transference issues that have not yet been identified?

REFERENCES

Acosta, F. X., Yamamoto, J., & Evans, L. (1982). *Effective psychotherapy for low-income and minority patients.* New York: Plenum.

Basch, M. F. (1986). Can this be psychoanalysis? In A. Goldberg (Ed.), *Progress in self psychology,* Vol. 2, pp. 18–30. New York: The Gulford Press.

Benedek, E. (1973). Training the woman resident to be a psychiatrist. *American Journal of Psychiatry, 130*(11), 1131–1135.

Chang, W. (1987). *Empathy: A cross-cultural encounter.* Paper presented at the Interactive Forum on Transference and Empathy in Psychotherapy with Asian Americans, South Cove Community Health Center and University of Massachusetts, Boston, MA.

Chin, J. L. (1981). Institutional racism and mental health: An Asian-American perspective. In O. A. Barbarin el al. (Eds.), *Institutional racism and community competence.* Washington, DC: U.S. Government Printing Office.

———— (1987, April). *Culture and Psychotherapy: Towards developing a multicultural framework.* Paper presented at the Annual Meeting of the Massachusetts Psychological Association, Boston, MA.

Comas-Diaz, L., & Minrath, M. (1985). Psychotherapy with ethnic minority borderline clients. *Psychotherapy, 22*(2). 418–426.

De La Cancela, V. (1985). Toward a sociocultural psychotherapy for low-income minorities. *Psychotherapy, 22*(2), 427–435.

Dewald, P. A. (1971). Transference. *Psychotherapy: A dynamic approach* (pp. 196–223). New York: Basic Books.

Dudley, G. R., & Rawlins, M. R. (Eds.). (1985). Psychotherapy with ethnic minorities. *Psychotherapy* [Special issue], *22*(2).

Freud, S. (1915). Observations on transference love. In J. Strachey (Ed.), *Complete Psychological Works of Sigmund Freud,* Vol. 12, pp. 157–171. London: Hogarth Press.

Gardner, L. (1980). Racial, ethnic and social class considerations in psychotherapy supervision. In A. Hess (Ed.), *Psychotherapy supervision: Theory, research and practice.* New York: Wiley.

Gilligan, C. (1982). *In a different voice.* Cambridge, MA: Harvard University Press.

Giovacchini, P. L. (1972). *Tactics and techniques in psychoanalytic therapy.* N.L.: Science House.

Gornick, L. (1986). Developing a new narrative: The woman therapist and the male patient. *Psychoanalytic Psychology, 3,* 299–325.

Greenson, R. (1965). The working alliance and the transference neurosis. *Psychoanalytic Quarterly, 34,* 155–181.

Greenson, R., Toney, E., Lim. P., & Romero, A. (1982). Transference and countertransference in interracial psychotherapy. In B. A. Bass, G. E. Wyatt, & G. J. Powell (Eds.), *The Afro-American family: Assessment, treatment and research issues.* New York: Grune & Stratton.

Greenson, R., & Wexler, M. (1969). The non-transference relationship in the psychoanalytic situation. *International Journal of Psychoanalysis, 50,* 27–40.

Hall, E. T. (1976). How cultures collide. *Psychology Today,* July, 66–97.

Ibrahim, F. A. (1985). Effectiveness in cross-cultural counseling and psychotherapy: A framework. *Psychotherapy,* 22 (2), 321–323.

Iwasaki, T. (1971). Discussion. In G. Ticho, Cultural Aspects of Transference and Countertransference. *Bulletin of the Menninger Clinic,* 35(5), 330–334.

Kim, S. C. (1985). Family therapy for Asian Americans: A strategic structural framework. *Psychotherapy* [Special issue: Psychotherapy with ethnic minorities]. 22(2), 342–348.

Kohut, H. (1971). *The Analysis of the self.* New York: International Universities Press.

Langs, R. (1974). *Technique of psychoanalytic psychotherapy,* Vol. 2. New York Aronson.

————— (1978). The patient's view of the therapist: Reality or fantasy? In R. Langs, *Technique in transition,* pp. 115–138. New York: Aronson.

McGoldrick, M., Pearce, J. K., & Giordano, J. (1982). *Ethnicity and Family Therapy.* New York: The Guilford Press.

Minuchin, S. (1974). *Families and Family Therapy.* Cambridge, MA: Harvard University Press.

Mogul, K. (1982). Overview: The sex of the therapist. *American Journal of Psychiatry, 129*(1), 1–11.

Stolorow, R. D. (1986). On experiencing an object: A multidimensional perspective. In A. Goldberg (Ed.), *Progress in self psychology,* Vol. 2, pp. 273–279. New York: The Guilford Press.

Sue, D. W. (1978). World views and counseling. *Personnel and Guidance Journal, 56,* 458–462.

Sue S. (1982). Ethnic minority issues in psychology. *American Psychologist, 38*(5), 583–592.

Sue, S., & Morishima, J. K. (1982). *The mental health of Asian Americans.* San Francisco: Jossey-Bass.

Suh, C. (1987). *The role of the psychotherapist with Asian clients: Toward transcending the hierarchical relationship.* Paper presented at the Interactive Forum on Transference and Empathy in Psychotherapy with Asian Americans, South Cove Community Health Center and University of Massachusetts, Boston, MA.

Thomas, A., & Sillen, S. (1972). *Racism and psychiatry.* New York: Brunner/Mazel.

Tjeltveit, A. C. (1989). The ubiquity of models of human beings in psychotherapy: The need for rigorous reflection. *Psychotherapy, 26* (1), 1–10.

Toupin, E. (1980). Counseling Asians: Psychotherapy in the context of racism and Asian American history. *American Journal of Orthopsychiatry, 50*(1), 76–86.

Tseng, W. (1973). The concept of personality in Confucian thought. *Psychiatry, 36,* 191–202

Wong, H. (1987). *Therapeutic alliances and Asian Americans: Aspects of Transference and Relationship in Psychotherapy.* Paper presented at the Interactive Forum on Transference and Empathy in Psychotherapy with Asian Americans, South Cove Community Health Center and University of Massachusetts, Boston, MA.

Wu, D. Y. H. (1987). *Achieving intra-cultural and inter-cultural understanding in psychotherapy with Asian* Americans. Paper presented at the Interactive Forum on Transference and Empathy in Psychotherapy with Asian Americans, South Cove Community Health Center and University of Massachusetts, Boston, MA.

Yamamoto, J., & Chang, C. (1987). *Empathy for the family and the individual in the social context.* Paper presented at the Interactive Forum on Transference and Empathy in Psychotherapy with Asian Americans, South Cove Community Health Center and University of Massachusets, Boston, MA.

Yamamoto, J., James, Q., & Palley, N. (1968) Cultural problems in psychiatric therapy. *General Archives of Psychiatry,* 19, 45–49.

Zaphiropoulos, M. L. (1982). Transcultural parameters in the transference and countertransference. *Journal of the American Academy of Psychoanalysis, 10*(4). 571–584.

3

Empathy

MaryAnna Domokos-Cheng Ham

Therapists must be persistent in attending to the interpersonal processes between their clients and themselves. It may be difficult to initiate or maintain the relationship even though both parties may desire it. As therapists, we must assume primary responsibility for these interrelationships, which are even more complex when our clients come from cultural traditions different from our own.

As therapists trained in the Western tradition, we are even more aware of the complexity of dealing with Asian clients, for we are immediately uncertain whether our standard methods of establishing a relationship are adequate. Often we feel as though we are traveling through a strange country with an incomplete map. We wonder whether knowing more about the nature of this unknown terrain might make the journey comfortable. We wonder, too, whether there is some bridge or conduit that will lead us securely from our own territory into this unknown terrain. We might wish for skills and tools to enable us to create a bridge between our Asian clients and ourselves.

Although the desire to understand others is most likely universal, Asian and Western sociocultural traditions provide unique instructions for how to express interpersonal behaviors and mold the meaning given to those behaviors. Beyond our universal desire to understand one another is a desire to communicate to others our understanding of them. As part of this communication we look for recognition in others that our understanding of them is somewhat accurate and acceptable to them. The specific behaviors to express this interaction of "understanding"and "being understood" may be different in every culture. The challenge of cross-cultural interaction, then, is for individuals of different traditions to express their "understanding" and "being understood" in ways that each one recognizes. In cross-cultural therapy both the therapist and the client are searching for some vehicle for understanding the maps each brings to the therapy session.

Empathy is viewed within Western psychotherapy as an essential vehicle for acquiring a map of the client's terrain, a way of establishing a fundamental connection that enables a successful therapeutic relationship. Empathic skills become a resource for therapists to use to connect their thoughts, feelings, and behaviors to the different interactional styles of a client from another culture.

It is important to emphasize that empathy is a Western concept. Chinese and Japanese dictionaries describe empathy as a newly coined word that has been borrowed from Western languages (Yamamoto & Chang, 1987). Yet, broadly speaking, the desire to understand, to feel along with, to anticipate another's behavior, or to predict what another will do is universal, even though members of Asian and Western cultures employ very different behaviors in the effort to achieve and convey understanding of another person.

When we speak of empathy we are talking about a process of giving personal and social meaning to a behavior within a specific cultural context. Yet, even within a specific cultural context, we must adopt multiple perspectives in order to define and implement the concept of empathy. By embracing multiple points of view we are better able to accept the similarities and differences between ourselves and others. The need to adopt multiple perspectives, is, in fact, evident in the definition of empathy, a concept that has many different meanings in Western culture (Gladstein and Assoc., 1987; Goldstein & Michaels, 1985). In Asian cultures, references to empathy actually more closely approximate the Western concept of sympathy, to be concerned about another (Yamamoto & Chang, 1987). These different ways of thinking about empathy reflect basic differences in Western and Asian cultures in how social, emotional, and cognitive experiences of all sorts are described and understood (White & Marsella, 1982). To understand, genuinely, the social, emotional, and cognitive experiences of others we must understand how they are interpreted within the cultural context in which they occur.

INTRODUCTION TO THE CONCEPT OF EMPATHY

Understanding: A Fundamental Component of Empathy

Cultural symbols and their meanings contribute to how we understand the emotions and behaviors of another person. We learn the meaning of these symbols and the importance they play in our lives as we develop emotionally and cognitively (Flavell, Botkin, Fry, Wright, & Jarvis, 1968). Throughout our growth from infancy to adulthood, we are taught to pay attention to specific aspects of our internal experiences and to those external events around us. In addition we are given symbols to label our internal and external experiences. Our understanding of these experiences falls into two continua and depends upon what data we are taught to focus upon and how we are to attend to those data. The first continuum identifies the experiences we are taught to focus upon and understand, and the second continuum describes how we attend to our experiences and understand them. From these continua come the symbols we must know in order to identify our experiences and the mechanisms to communicate our understanding of them. The polarities of the first continuum are our intrapsychic and interpersonal experiences; the second continuum defines as polarities the affective and cognitive mechanisms we use for understanding ourselves and each other and for communicating our understanding.

On the intrapsychic-interpersonal continuum, intrapsychic is defined as an internal process through which we know, comprehend, or perceive what others are experiencing. If we focus on the internal process of others, we become aware of their unique responses to their own environment, including both their internal domain and the world external to them. From this perspective, we acknowledge the separateness of others from us as we attend to how they interpret their own internal process (Buie, 1981; Kohut, 1977). At the interpersonal end of this continuum, our experiences of other people rely upon an interactive process in which we and another person affect each other. This interpersonal process is shaped by cultural and social events that affect our assumptions about the person involved with us in the interactive process (White & Marsella, 1982). In our relationships with other people, the inferences we make about them evolve from a framework provided by our own society and culture. The methods we use to engage them in an interactive process also develop from our relationships to others in our own society and culture (Howell, 1977; Neisser, 1976).

The second continuum, in addition to the affective-cognitive polarities, has a midpoint where these two mechanisms for understanding and communicating coexist. When we engage affective aspects of ourself in an interpersonal interaction, our understanding of the other person is close to an emotional identification with him or her (Rogers, 1951). We are attuned, even without conscious awareness, to the feelings and emotions the other person may express either verbally or nonverbally. Our reactions to the verbal and nonverbal cues of the other person are often automatic and unconscious. On the other end of this continuum, our understanding of the other person draws on our ability to organize the data we acquire as we interact with and observe him or her. We use prior knowledge about human interactions as a foundation for knowing or predicting what another person is thinking or feeling (Howell, 1977; Neisser, 1976).

These two continua are interdependent. Our intrapsychic and interpersonal experiences of another person draw upon our own self-awareness, which, in turn, requires use of our own feeling or affective states and cognitive skills. Our efforts to understand another person involve both introspective observations and social perceptions.

Empathy: Process, Trait, and Skill

Empathy further expands upon the term *understanding* by elaborating upon the distinction between observation and interaction (Basch, 1983; Buie, 1984). Within the frameworks of self psychology, role theory, and communication theory, empathy "is unanimously viewed as an interpersonal mode of observation applied to psychological events" (Buie, 1984, p. 129). These theories emphasize the influence of the interactional process occurring between two or more individuals and suggest mutual involvement, influence, and alterations between the participants in the process (Ham, 1987b).

In an empathic process, the participants are able to "observe" themselves in an introspective process as well as "observe" the full range of experiences of the other person participating in the interaction. Although empathy depends fundamentally on inference (Buie, 1981), we "understand" the inner life of other persons by observing their behaviors as a cue to their inner state of being (Buie, 1984). The meaning we give to the behavioral cues is affected by how we label and categorize behaviors (White & Marsella, 1982). However, any interpersonal process requires at least two people who affect each other. In certain interpersonal interactions we are capable of modifying or expanding our inferred assumptions about the meaning of the other person's behavior. In some instances we find we cannot emotionally tolerate the behavioral cues the other person offers, such as those we might perceive as hostile, angry behaviors (Ham, 1987b). In other instances the behavioral cues the other person displays may not be within our cognitive range of knowledge or within our awareness of certain categories of behaviors.

The mechanisms for observing another person in an empathic process have not been clearly delineated and "controversy arises about the nature of the 'observing' mechanism" (Buie, 1984, p. 129). Although empathy has been thought of as an innate trait, part of basic human endowment (Kohut, 1977), it has also been determined to be a cognitive skill that is learned (Feshbach, 1978; Flavell et al., 1968; Sarbin & Allen, 1969). Whether empathy is an innate human trait or a learned skill, the implication is that our ability to be empathic affects our capability to understand another human being. The assertion that empathy is more effective when two people share the same culture (Kohut, 1977) implies that the inferences necessary in understanding the behavioral cues of the other person often are derived from similar social and cultural experiences. However, emotional identification may not be the same as empathic identification (Rogers, 1951). The distinction is important. Two people who can identify and share an emotional experience with each other do not necessarily describe the experience in similar ways. A further refinement of this distinction is to acknowledge the difference between perceiving the emotions and events of another person through intellectual and thoughtful reflection on the interaction and experiencing those same feelings and events as if they were actually your own. This distinction acknowledges the contributions of both mechanisms, innate traits and learned skills, to the total process required of us when we use our empathic ability.

EMPATHY IN THE WESTERN TRADITION OF PSYCHOTHERAPY

Western psychotherapy conceives of empathy in three ways: as an innate trait the therapist brings to psychotherapy with a client, as a skill that can be taught to a therapist prior to the encounter with a client, and as a process involving the interaction between a therapist and a client during a therapy session.

Empathy as a Trait

Therapists often draw upon their own emotional resources, their own affective and intrapsychic understanding, in order to have an emotional response to their clients. This affective and intrapsychic dimension of empathy has been described as an intuitive and emotional response of one person resonating to another person's feelings in much the same way we have the capacity as part of our human endowment to see and hear another person (Kohut, 1977).

Confusion lies in any declaration that our emotional response to our patients is *only* a trait and is not dependent upon a process where one person recognizes and identifies with the emotional experiences of the other person (Buie, 1981; Gladstein,1983; Goldstein & Michaels, 1985). Our ability, as therapists, to perceive the inner experiences of our clients through physiological mimicry, affective reverberation, and faithful reproduction of nonverbal and verbal cues depends upon personal interactions (Goldstein & Michaels, 1985). In addition, the psychological phenomena of merging and identification, also related to our ability to perceive the inner experiences of our clients (Buie, 1981), rely upon inter-personal relationships. Kohut (1966) regards merging as "import-ant to primitive, infantile empathy where primary empathy with mother prepares us for recognition that, to a large extent, the basic inner experiences of people remain similar to our own" (p. 262). Identification indicates some relationship between a person's own self-experience and the subjective experience of another. In the emotional development of a person, "a path leads from identifica-tion by way of imitation to empathy, that is, to the comprehension of the mechanism by means of which we are enabled to take up any attitude at all toward another mental life" (Freud, 1923, p. 110).

Sympathy, a concept related to empathy but more closely asso-ciated with condolence, pity, and agreement, emphasizes height-ened attention to one's own feelings and assumes a kind of internal reverberation. In sympathy, we assume a similarity between the feelings of both the person who is sympathetic and the person who stimulates the feelings (Goldstein & Michaels, 1985; Katz, 1963). Both projection (an unconscious attribution of one's desires or wishes) and identification (an unconscious modeling of oneself in thought, feeling, or action after another person) are examples of sympathy where a person is preoccupied with his or her own feelings in response to another person.

As our discussion of empathy continues and we begin to juxtapose the meaning of empathy in the Western and Asian traditions, we will emphasize the contrast between sympathy and empathy. Both empathy and sympathy, as intuitive traits, require us to draw upon our own emotional resources in responding sensitively to the ongoing emotional world of another person. However, empathy focuses attention on the feelings and context of the other person, rather than only on our own internal state (Katz, 1963). When we are sympathetic we understand the other person because of an awareness of our own internal state; when we are empathic we go beyond our own emotional awareness and use information we have acquired in our conversation with them. If we only intuit what the other person feels without inquiring from the other person whether our intuition is accurate, then we have sympathized with the other person. If we notice that our intuition of the other person may not be exactly what he or she is experiencing, yet experience the other's feelings, we are empathic. In Western psychotherapy we try to empathize with our clients rather than only intuit or sympathize with them. We distance ourselves enough so we can listen and include the other person's perceptions of his or her own feeling and experience.

Empathy as a Skill

Using cognition as a basis for empathic understanding of clients requires therapists to develop predictive and inferential skills. These skills are acquired as part of an individual's cognitive development (Bieri, 1961; Bronfenbrenner, Harding, & Gallway, 1968; Flavell et al., 1968). As a predictive skill, empathy involves creating inferential strategies even in the absence of the other person (Chandler, 1974).

Again we must note that empathy as a skill involves a process and relies upon the interactive nature of the concept. To succeed in using our empathic skill, we need to draw inferences from cues presented to us and form hypotheses or working models about another person's point of view and experience. But we must also be vigilant regarding how our clients respond to our empathic skill. If a client does not respond to our initial efforts, we must draw upon our empathic skill and modify our empathic behavior. This highly complex cognitive process is demanded from us when we undertake the process of psychotherapy with clients whose knowledge base and experiences are different from our own. Yet, empathy, even though it has been determined to be a necessary therapeutic skill, still may not be the only skill therapists need to learn in order for therapy to occur (Gladstein, 1970, 1977, 1983; Rogers, 1951; Truax & Carkhuff, 1967).

Whether separating empathic responses into affective traits and cognitive skills is a piecemeal approach to personality and behavioral organization has been highly debated (Chandler, 1974). Intuitively, we often feel that limiting how we predict the feelings and behaviors of others to a cognitive skill does not take into consideration the affective projection of an individual's own feelings onto another person (Chandler, 1974). However, the distinction between the components of empathy has been recognized, even though the exact degrees of difference between affective and cognitive empathic dimensions have not been determined (Ham, 1987a). One conclusion from Ham's (1987a) research is that both affective and cognitive skills, in some capacity and combination, contribute to our empathic ability. The way we combine our affective and cognitive skills is shaped by personal experiences within a social and cultural environment (Feshbach, 1978). Yet, we all experience in some balance these three elements of empathy: (1) to be able to recognize and discriminate affective states in another; (2) to be able to assume the perspective, role, and affect of another; and (3) to have the affective responsiveness and capacity necessary to empathize (Feshbach, 1978; Yamamoto & Chang, 1987).

Empathy as a Process

One important function of empathy in psychotherapy is to establish a therapeutic relationship between therapists and their clients. Because the relationship between therapists and clients entails "a special way of being" with another person (Rogers, 1975), therapists need to be aware of this "special way of being" as a relational process of "stepping into the shoes" of the clients. This relational process is not merely an action-oriented behavior but requires us to offer relational characteristics such as warmth, nonjudgmental understanding, and positive regard to our clients (Rogers, 1975). The task of understanding our clients involves a process in which each of us begins to develop trust. Our clients in the therapeutic relationship, in order to have confidence in our skill to establish a relationship with them, must perceive us as trustworthy (Brammer & Shostrom, 1968). Mutual trust creates an environment where the therapeutic process is a "joint effort."

Empathy is a reciprocal process in which the client and therapist need to have both cognitive understanding and affective sensitivity toward each other (Ham, 1987b). Being able to take the role of our clients requires intensive interaction with them and is actually a reciprocal process where one person steps into the shoes of the other (Mead, 1935; Sarbin & Allen, 1969). The relationship between actors and their audience offers a good example of how role-taking behavior is a reciprocal process. Notably, actors not only perform to an audience by predicting or inferring empathically what the audience expects from them but also their performance aims at meeting the expectations and the needs of the audience (Hogan, 1975).

Our empathic behavior during a psychotherapy session contributes to and facilitates the relationship between us and our clients. Our empathic ability, reflecting an innate trait or a learned skill, does not necessarily lead to a helping or to therapeutic behavior

(Egan, 1990; Gladstein & Assoc., 1987; Ham, 1987b; Hoffman, 1977). In the therapeutic process, accurate empathy involves more than just our ability to sense clients' private worlds as if these worlds were our own and more than our ability to understand cognitively or emotionally what our clients mean. Accurate empathy is the degree to which we are successful in communicating our awareness and understanding of the client's current feelings in language attuned to that client (Lambert, DeJulio, & Stein, 1978).

Accurate communication of empathy involves a multistep therapeutic process: (1) perceiving overt behaviors of the client, verbal and nonverbal; (2) accurately understanding the meanings of the client; (3) experiencing affective responses to the client's messages while remaining as free as possible from cognitive distortion such as stereotyping and value judgments; (4) separating feelings shared with the client from those held alone; and (5) accurately communicating feelings back to clients so that they feel understood (Keefe, 1976), which is considered the final stage of empathic understanding (Keefe,1976; Rogers 1957, 1975; Truax & Carkhuff, 1967). In engaging clients in the therapeutic process, we need to go beyond predictive empathy, our awareness and understanding of clients, and beyond emotional resonance with them. We must be able to communicate both our emotional and cognitive understanding of clients in a language that is familiar to them. They must sense, know, and feel that we understand and empathize with them.

EMPATHY IN THE ASIAN TRADITION

The expression of empathy in Asian cultures has a long history and is thought of as an attitude based upon an operationalized philosophy about human nature and as a set of rules to be learned and used as social skills. Although guidelines for interpersonal behavior exist in all cultures as myths and metaphors expressed in folk stories, religious parables, and fairy tales, Asian myths and metaphorical stories are unique to Asian culture and have specific meanings. In understanding empathy in the Asian tradition we must become acquainted with the meanings of Asian myths and stories and the lessons to be learned from them. Empathy is taught through the paradigms of Asian religions and the metaphors expressed in traditional stories and fairy tales. In traditional religious and folk stories important to Asian culture, empathy, sympathy, and other related behaviors such as compassion, generosity, and kindheartedness are described as components of an ethical code for living that must be followed or misfortune will ensue (Yamamoto & Chang, 1987).

For Asians who have learned about interpersonal behavior through their social experiences in a family, among friends, and perhaps in an established community of Asians, empathic behavior is a common human interaction that is manifested as caring and concern for others. Asians learn in their development from infancy to adulthood the behaviors that connote caring and concern for others.

Empathy as a Code for Living

The ancient and complex philosophical and religious traditions of Buddhism, Confucianism, and Taoism provide the basis for understanding the Asian meaning of empathy. These philosophical traditions provide codes for living or instructions for offering caring, concern, and empathy for fellow human beings (Yamamoto & Chang, 1987). Embedded in each of these religious-philosophical traditions are descriptions of behaviors similar to the Western concept of sympathy: an intuitive, affective awareness of the other person that is based upon your own sensitivity to the emotional world of yourself. Since the demonstration of the Asian concept of empathy is to respond to the other person without asking them to verbalize explicitly their emotional state of being, a caring response to other people requires an intuitive awareness of their emotional state. In order to assist a person to be caring, explicit codes of living are set forth as a guide for responding to the emotional states of the other person as well as to the emotions within oneself that have been generated by the other person.

Buddhism. In early Buddhist writings of the fifth and sixth centuries B.C., concepts of loving kindness and great compassion were denoted by several words. In Theravada Buddhism the word *anukampa* can be literally translated to mean"being moved in accordance with others" (Aronson, 1980). Aronson (1980) translated this word as "sympathy." The word *upaya*, from Mahayana Buddhism, the school of Buddhism that spread to China, Japan, and Korea, was used for "love and compassion," an equivalent to *anukampa*, or "sympathy" (Yamamoto, 1982).

Confucianism. Confucius (551–479 B.C.), a philosopher who had a great influence on Chinese thinking, followed the precept of human heartedness, a concept close to empathy. In this context, empathy was actually a behavior like sympathy where man was considered a social creature bound to his fellow man by *ren* or human heartedness. To understand *ren*, or human heartedness, is to be aware that the Chinese character for *ren* means two persons. Thus, *ren* can only be cultivated and developed in relationships between people in a social context (King & Bond, 1985; Lin, 1974/1975). In terms of social interaction, Confucius outlined an ideal society as a complicated role system where harmonious social interactions were treasured as the highest social value (King & Bond, 1985). In Confucian social philosophy, the individual was never conceived of as an isolated, separate entity: man was a social or interactive being and was defined as part of an interaction (Moore, 1967). Social interactions were defined through five relationships: sovereign and subject, parent and child, elder and younger brother, husband and wife, and friend and friend. These relationships were regulated by *li*, the term used for the set of rules, etiquette, and ritual that made relationships function smoothly. Man, a player of roles in relationships prescribed by *li*, was a relational being who was to honor yet be "sensitive" to relations with others.

Taoism. Taoism began in the third century B.C. The central belief in Taoism is that there is a natural flow and progression of life to death, yang to yin, from spring to summer to fall to winter, and also from the yin to yang, and death to life. In the yin-yang five-element theory, human attributes are all interrelated, and the movements of these interactions are then reflected in the body of man. Implicit in this theory is an understanding and "sensitivity" to the balance of the attributes: benevolence, propriety, faith, righteousness, and wisdom (Yamamoto & Chang, 1987).

Empathy as an Interpersonal and Social Skill

The basis for empathy within Asian tradition is the interdependence of family members. One example of the closeness of family ties is the traditional sleeping arrangement of the Japanese family, with mats laid in one area and set around the mother and father. The youngest child is placed closest to the mother, the next youngest in the adjacent position, and so on. In this tradition, strong bonds, a special relationship, and a longer period of interdependence are established between the Japanese mother and her children.

Yamamoto and Chang (1987) concluded, after reviewing a series of studies exploring how empathy is learned in the developmental process, that children across cultures seem to be empathic at quite a young age. They noted, however, that early socialization processes are essential in the development of empathy and account for important cross-cultural differences in its expression For example, data from Helen Borke's study (1973) concluded that middle-class Chinese children were able to identify fearful situations at 3 years old, a younger age than their American counterparts, who caught up in this ability by age 4 to 4 ½ . This conclusion suggests that the existence of interdependent relationships between Chinese children and their parents is important in the development of empathy in China, whereas peer socialization contributes significantly to the development of empathy in American children (Yamamoto & Chang, 1987). This possible interpretation emphasizes the importance of the Confucian theme: Children's misbehavior is the fault of the family unit, which is chiefly responsible for socializing its members. Chinese children who are learning the implication of this Confucian teaching begin to recognize and respond to sad situations earlier in order to "protect themselves and their family through face-saving or not losing face and being shamed" as a way of justifying the behavior of another family member. This behavior seen in the early development of children is sympathy: an identification of the emotional state of the other person by an identification of their own feelings. In contrast, Borke (1973) concluded that American children improved in their perception of sadness between the ages of 4 and 6 as a result of increased socialization among their peers, who at this age were able to express verbally to one another what their feelings were.

For both Asian and Western children, empathy is a social skill learned from family and community members, who teach them a set of rules for interpreting and evaluating themselves in social experiences. Sets of rules to live by are learned through a child's experience within a social context. Social skills, whether they be caring and concern, sympathy or empathy, must be learned through the filters, the personal and social schemata, offered by the society.

However, for Asians, the set of rules taught to children by family members and maintained by the Asian community and culture emphasizes that caring and concern for others not only evolves from a social experience but that caring and concern for others must support and maintain a functional social structure. Humane and compassionate behavior is expressed as a demonstration of sympathetic caring for the community. For example, rebellious children are encouraged to adjust their behavior to meet the concerns of the family and community rather than to think only of what they feel is best for them.

Empathy as expressed in this demonstrated concern for society is frequently conveyed through metaphor. A traditional Chinese fairy tale called the "Magic Pear Tree" is an example of how the social skill of empathy is represented in the metaphorical content of fairy tales. The tale is as follows: A farmer comes from the country to sell his pears in the market. A Taoist priest wearing tattered clothes begs for some fruit, but the farmer refuses. A crowd gathers to persuade the farmer to give the priest a bruised pear, but the farmer continues adamantly to refuse. A guard standing nearby buys the priest a piece of fruit. Taking the pear, the priest then says,

"We who have left the world find man's greed hard to understand. Let me offer some choice pears to all you good customers." With that, he eats the pear and plants the seed. A tree magically sprouts, grows tall, blooms, and bears fruit in front of the crowd and the farmer. The priest harvests the pears and passes them around. Having done that, he chops down the tree and leaves. When the priest leaves, the farmer notices that the pears given away by the priest were his own fruit. The lesson of this fairy tale is to be aware of the individualistic concerns and greed of the farmer, who is punished for not demonstrating humanitarian and compassionate behavior toward the community. The guard, through his empathic response to the priest, benefits the community. This fairy tale portrays kindheartedness and generosity and teaches, through symbolic meanings, the value of empathy in Asian society and culture.

The lesson of this fairy tale contrasts with those of Western myths and fairy tales. In the culture of the United States, where many religious, ethnic, and racial groups are represented, the metaphors are diverse. Yet, the metaphor of the "Western Frontier" prevails as the folk myth. The belief that each individual is capable of venturing into and conquering unknown territory is a dominant theme. The Western "cowboy" searches for independence without considering community or society, while the protagonist of the Asian fairy tale demonstrates humanitarian behavior toward the community.

USING EMPATHY AS A BRIDGE BETWEEN ASIAN CLIENTS AND WESTERN PSYCHOTHERAPY

As psychotherapists we use every aspect of our personhood to engage our client in a therapeutic relationship. We bring to the therapy session all of our skills and our personality to use as tools in therapy (Brammer & Shostrom, 1968). Empathy, our capacity to feel and to understand the feelings and experiences of others, is part of our human endowment and is a cognitive skill that can be developed. Empathy becomes a bridge connecting us with our clients. When we, as therapists trained in a Western tradition, encounter Asian clients, we bring to the therapeutic relationship our capacity to feel the feelings of our clients and our ability to observe and think abstractly about their experiences. We must also be able to communicate to our clients that we understand their feelings and and their experiences. This entire process of feeling along with our clients, of understanding intellectually their experiences, and communicating back to them, so they know we understand them, is empathy as it is practiced in psychotherapy. In psychotherapy with Asian clients our empathic behavior takes on a special importance, for we depend upon a "bridge" to help us to connect with feelings and experiences that may initially appear to be very different from ours. In order for us to develop fully our empathic "bridge" to Asian clients, we must incorporate the multiple dimensions of empathy: empathy as a trait, a skill, and a process.

Empathy as a Trait

Societies and cultures have distinct ways of labeling emotions and behaviors. These labels are not merely words, for members of each society and culture understand, in using the label, the manner in which the emotion or behavior is to be expressed (White & Marsella, 1982). Regardless of these labels, we often find ourselves responding spontaneously to strong emotions in our clients (Buie, 1981). "When [clients] are about to express or actually express strong feelings or impulses, [therapists] may experience a similar feeling at a level of intensity exceeding that involved in self-experienced reference" (Buie, 1981, p. 297). This sharing of feelings does not necessarily lead to an accurate understanding of the client's feelings. Often, the meaning of the client's behavior and feelings is misunderstood, just as there is frequent misunderstanding of the client's expression of the behavior or feeling. However, even when misunderstanding the emotions, the therapist has a "sense" of some emotional expression of the client.

Regardless of any obvious differences from our clients, such as race, ethnicity, or gender, we are able to respond to strongly felt emotion in our Asian clients because we are experiencing the client's feelings within ourselves. This shared emotional experience, as empathic resonance, leads us to an experience emphasizing an intuitive awareness of another person. This intuitive experience Asians call sympathy. Our ability to be introspective, a component of the Western experience of empathy, heightens our sensitivity to the emotions of our Asian clients and highlights our intuitive awareness of another person. Whether we call intuitive awareness empathy or sympathy is a matter of labeling. When we use the traits of empathy and sympathy with our Asian clients, we are concerned, not with how our emotional response to the client is labeled but with our actual emotional resonance or "sense" of the client.

Empathy as a Skill

As therapists our capability to know the feelings of our Asian clients evolves not only from our emotional resonance with them as fellow human beings but also from our cognitive awareness of their social and cultural experiences.

Understanding between individuals of different societies must include and perhaps emphasize the cognitive component of empathy. In the interaction between Western-trained psychotherapists and Asian clients, each of whom has different social schemata, the cognitive processes involved in taking-in, processing, and communicating information are of central importance (Chang, 1987). Normal everyday perception is a kind of hypothesis-testing or inferential thinking where everyone involved in a social interaction tests out hypotheses generated by their own cognitive structure (Chang, 1987). In the process of social interactions, and specifically in the therapy process where therapists and clients have cognitively learned different ways to express emotion and to conceptualize social experiences, both therapists and clients must modify their cognitive structures if they are to accommodate new information. This modification then becomes the basis for predictive empathy, an important component for Western-trained therapists to perceive experiences of their Asian clients and for Asian clients to feel understood. Cognitive processes enable both therapists and clients with different social experiences to become known to each other. Specifically, therapists who have learned through reading or interpersonal experiences about the cognitive structures of their Asian clients will acknowledge that a demonstration of concern for their Asian clients may take different forms of expression and, thus, they can communicate empathy in a way their Asian clients can understand.

Affected by our own interpersonal experiences, we often predict or make inferences about our Asian clients before we engage in a therapeutic relationship with them. In any interpersonal process, we rely upon inference to anticipate what the other person may feel or how they may behave. In this predictive process, prior to our encounter with Asian clients, we do not alter our expectations of the client. Only as we interact with our Asian clients do we begin to learn the meaning of their behavioral cues. At this point of connection we can begin to step into their shoes as we refine our own cognitive structures. To refine our cognitive understanding of our Asian client can be learned as a skill or tool for understanding someone whose cognitive structure is different from our own.

The following observation made by a Japanese psychiatric sociologist (Munakata, 1986) and later described by Wu (1987) is an example of how a Western-trained psychotherapist could have benefited from the skill of predictive empathy. A male Japanese American client refused to open up and engage in a relationship with his Western psychotherapist because the therapist would not let him indulge himself in the way a Japanese child is indulged by a parent (*amaeru*). The patient felt that the therapist made no efforts to establish emotional ties with him and, therefore, could not be trusted. No language issue was involved, for the patient spoke perfect English. To establish the therapeutic relationship and to be empathic to his client, the Western psychotherapist needed to understand the two most important factors in Japanese culture:

amae and *sassuru*. *Amae*, the parent's indulgence of a child, needed to be played out by the "doctor" or psychotherapist behaving like a father and encouraging the client to depend on him. The psychotherapist, as part of *amae*, would be able to *sassuru*, to "guess" and understand the client's feelings without relying on verbal communication. Regardless of whether the therapist spoke Japanese or English or whether the therapist was Asian or non-Asian, the client would feel dissatisfied and mistrustful if the therapist did not demonstrate understanding of *amae* and *sassuru* (Wu, 1987).

Belief systems are embedded in every culture and are used by the members of a society as cognitive tools to perceive, categorize, and make sense of their world (White, 1982). As therapists whose belief systems may differ from those of our Asian clients, we need to be respectful and highly aware of different beliefs and values. Our first step in understanding different values and beliefs is to instruct ourselves about the belief systems of our Asian clients through numerous cognitive experiences such as reading books, attending lectures and workshops, and discussing information with colleagues. Most important, however, we instruct ourselves about our clients from the clients themselves. We listen nonjudgmentally, respectfully, and without preconceived notions, for we come to the therapy session as students.

Empathy as a Process

A Cultural Process. The interactional process where empathy takes place can be understood in terms of underlying assumptions drawn from a cultural experience (Wu, 1987). One common assumption about culture is that it is learned behavior that can be acquired or understood through experience. However, many behavioral norms, conceptions, and symbolic representations are usually unconscious to individuals in a particular culture (Wu, 1987). For Western-trained therapists this unconscious acceptance of their own cultural norms may affect and even limit their understanding of their Asian clients. In addition, cultural empathy learned from conscious participation in social interactions may only amount to a superficial, remedial level of cultural reality (Wu, 1987). Cultural empathy, "stepping into" the culture of another person, is not a simple skill for therapists to learn, for intrapsychic feelings commonly experienced by individuals who live within the same culture develop from shared cultural experiences. The individuals within the same culture who experience similar feelings in response to shared cultural events are able, then, to engage in an intracultural empathic process (Wu, 1987). Yet, cultural empathy may be a learning process, an intercultural empathic process, as described from a traditional anthropological point of view, where understanding is acquired through consultation of literature and through observation of individuals in their social interactions and social groupings (Wu, 1987). In attempting to acquire intercultural empathy, Western-trained therapists are similar to respectful anthropologists.

One approach to integrating the intracultural and intercultural empathic process is to view culture as a subjective experience. Once again, as recommended in learning empathic skill, we must be respectful listeners and learn from Asian clients their own interpretations of their cultural experiences. We as listeners are then able to be culturally empathic.

Another method for understanding the cultural experience of Asian clients is by reading, analyzing, and contrasting cultural themes in Asian and Western myths and fairy tales. The contrast between Western fairy tales, where the adults, parents, and authority figures are depicted as evil and threatening, such as in *Hansel and Gretel, Snow White*, and *Cinderella*, and Chinese and Japanese fairy tales, where authority figures are often portrayed as understanding and kind (Yamamoto & Chang, 1987), is a contrast between cultural expectations and norms for behavior in each environment.

The importance of using an appropriate fairy tale as a metaphoric example is that Asian clients use Asian cultural metaphors in describing their own personal events, which are, in fact, meaningful stories about their cultural experiences. Stories written by Maxine Hong Kingston, Amy Tan, and Gish Jen are examples of how story telling becomes a metaphor for describing cultural and personal experiences.

A Communication Process. Empathic communication, an interactional skill, enables us to operationalize empathy in psychotherapy. Yamamoto (1982) coined the phrase "active empathy" to convey the Asian emphasis on communicating active appreciation of the other in an empathic process. This phrase suggests that therapists should not only be empathic with their Asian clients but should also communicate appreciation of all aspects of their clients' lives by trying to do something to be helpful (Yamamoto & Chang, 1987). Important to the therapy is the need for therapists to demonstrate directly that they can help their Asian clients by responding specifically to problems they present. For example, if a client asks for medication to eliminate symptoms created by his or her problem, then the therapist needs to provide a way for the client to receive medication. Active empathy assumes an understanding and a demonstration of reciprocity. This reciprocity is seen in the interaction of credibility and giving. For example, if by conceptualizing a client's problem in a manner consistent with the client's worldview a therapist gains credibility, then the client will more readily accept the care and concern the therapist offers (Sue & Zane, 1987).

Expression of empathy toward the family of one's clients is as important as communicating empathy to clients individually (Yamamoto & Chang, 1987), because you can demonstrate respect of Asian codes of living to both the client and the client's family. Your inclusion of the family will show your understanding of the Confucian value that people are interactive beings and are shaped in a relational context. By including the family in treatment, you can also listen to the family's explanation of their family culture and directly offer respect to the family members. This demonstration of empathy enables therapists to meet their clients on a culturally syntonic basis (Yamamoto & Chang, 1987). With family involvement, therapeutic gains may be aimed toward culturally syntonic goals such as cooperation rather than competition and interpersonal relationships rather than individualization (Yama-moto & Chang, 1987).

Another approach for communicating with clients is based upon recent thinking in anthropology (Wu, 1987). This approach suggests that clients need to be encouraged to explain their own interpretation of the social context affecting them. This approach to communicating caring and concern for clients is respectful of the differences between clients and therapists. It acknowledges that therapists need to learn from their clients and, thus, avoid their own ethnocentrism. Clients are given the voice and the power to name, interpret, and analyze their own life experiences (Wu, 1987). We learn our clients' perspective, regardless of how idiosyncratic or even distorted it may be. In turn, clients, in explaining their world, learn about themselves: their internal, social, and cultural experiences.

In the exchange between therapists and clients, one that requires cognitive and affective empathic understanding as well as empathic communication, a twofold process occurs: first, the therapist offers an invitation to the client to communicate, to inform, and to interpret; and second, the client senses that he or she is affecting the therapist's perceptions. Therapists offering empathic listening in this way accept their clients' own interpretations and conceptions of their world as the most insightful ones (Wu, 1987).

CONCLUSION

This chapter attempts to bring together the complexities of empathy from both a Western and an Asian perspective. Empathy, from both perspectives, involves a kind of understanding and concern for another person and is a crucial component of the therapeutic process. However, in psychotherapy therapists must go beyond an understanding of their clients. They must operationalize their understanding of clients and develop skill in communicating empathic understanding to the other person. For Western or Asian psychotherapists who have been trained in the Western tradition, it is essential in building relationships with Asian clients to develop the ability to be affectively sensitive, to learn information about the belief systems and cognitive structures of Asian clients, and to learn the skill of empathic communication. Developing these components of empathy is our first step in achieving a positive therapeutic outcome with Asian clients.

DISCUSSION QUESTIONS

1. The different authors referred to in this chapter approach the concept of empathy from different perspectives. What are the commonalities among them?

2. In conducting therapy with Asian Americans, is the distinction between predictive empathy (indirect or cognitive understanding) and active empathy (the communication of empathy) important to the outcome of treatment?

3. Can a distinction be made between affective and cognitive components in the empathic understanding a therapist has of an Asian American client?

4. To achieve empathic understanding of an Asian American client, how does a therapist incorporate concepts of self, role, and society/culture?

5. How can a therapist with her own sociocultural perspective achieve empathic understanding of an Asian American client?

6. Given the fact that therapist and client perceive and interpret the world from idiosyncratic internal knowledge structures, what steps should a therapist take to ensure his or her understanding of the client's reality?

7. What importance do language and cultural symbols, that is, perceptual and cognitive factors, have in the empathic interaction between client and therapist when one or both are Asian American?

8. How can methods of research used by anthropologists to understand the social, emotional and cognitive experiences of another culture be helpful in exploring the communication process between client and therapist of the same or different cultures?

9 How is the Asian emphasis on interdependence related to the issue of empathy? The point is made that the processes of interdependence and reciprocity are related to the communication of sympathy and

that this concept is understood in Eastern philosophy as empathy. Are sympathy and empathy, in fact, the same?

10. There is a fine line between cultural understanding and cultural stereotyping. How do therapists ensure they are making use of cultural understanding to achieve empathy?

REFERENCES

Aronson, H. B. (1980). *Love and sympathy in Theravada Buddhism.* Delhi: Motilal Banarsidassi.

Basch, M. F. (1983). Empathic understanding: A review of the concept and some theoretical considerations. *Journal of the American Psychoanalytic Association 31*(1), 101–126.

Bieri, J. (1961). Complexity–simplicity as a personality variable in cognitive and preferential behavior. In D. Fiske & S. Madd (Eds.), *Functions of varied experience.* Homewood, IL: The Dorsey Press.

Borke, H. (1973). The development of empathy in Chinese and American children between three and six years of age: A cross-culture study. *Developmental Psychology, 9*, 102–108.

Brammer, L. M., & Shostrom, E. L. (1968). *Therapeutic psychology* (2nd ed.). Englewood Cliffs, NJ: Prentice-Hall.

Bronfenbrenner, V., Harding, J., & Gallway, M. (1968). The measurement of skill in social perception. In D. McClelland, A. Baldwin, V. Bronfenbrenner, & F. Grodbeck (Eds.), *Talent and society* (pp. 29–111). Princeton, NJ: Van Nostrand.

Buie, D. (1981). Empathy: Its nature and limitations. *Journal of the American Psychoanalytic Association, 29*, 281–307.

————. (1984). Discussion. In J. Lichtenberg, M. Bornstein, & D. Silver (Eds.), *Empathy I* (pp. 129–136). Hillsdale, NJ: Lawrence Erlbaum Associates.

Chandler, M. J. (1974, September). *Accurate and accidental empathy.* Paper presented at the American Psychological Association meeting, New Orleans, LA.

Chang, W. C. (1987, August). *Empathy: A cross-cultural encounter.* Paper presented at the Interactive Forum on Transference and Empathy in Psychotherapy with Asian Americans, South Cove Community Health Center and University of Massachusetts, Boston, MA.

Egan, G. (1990). *The skilled helper: A systematic approach to effective helping* (4th ed.). Monterey, CA: Brooks/Cole.

Feshbach, N. D. (1978). Studies of empathic behavior in children. *Progress in Experimental Personality Research, 8,* 1–47.

Flavell, J. H., Botkin, P. T., Fry, C. L., Jr., Wright, J. W., & Jarvis, P. (1968). *The development of role-taking and communication skills in children.* New York: Wiley.

Freud, S. (1923). *Group psychology and the analysis of the ego.* New York: Boni and Liveright. (Original work published 1921.)

Gladstein, G. A. (1970). Is empathy important in counseling? *Personnel and Guidance Journal, 48*(10), 823–827.

———— . (1977). Empathy and counseling outcome: An empirical and conceptual review. *The Couseling Psychologist, 6*(4), 70–79.

———— . (1983). Understanding empathy: Integrating counseling, developmental and social psychology perspectives. *Journal of Counseling psychology,* 30(4), 467–482.

Gladstein, G. A. & Associates (Eds.). (1987). Empathy and counseling: Explorations in theory and research. New York: Springers Verlag.

Goldstein, A. P., & Michaels, G. Y. (1985). *Empathy: Development, training, and consequences.* Hillsdale, NJ: Lawrence Erlbaum.

Ham, M. D. (1987a). Counselor empathy. In G. A. Gladstein and Associates (Eds.), *Empathy and Counseling: Explorations in theory and research* (pp. 21–30). New York: Springer-Verlag.

———— . (1987b). Client behavior and counselor empathic performance. In G. A. Gladstein and Associates (Eds.), *Empathy and counseling: Explorations in theory and research* (pp. 31–50). New York: Springer-Verlag.

Hoffman, M. L. (1977). Empathy, its development and pro-social implications. *Nebraska Symposium on Motivation,* Vol. 25, pp. 169–218. University of Nebraska, Lincoln, NE.

Hogan, R. (1975). Empathy: A conceptual and psychometric analysis. *The Counseling Psychologist, 5*(2), 14–18.

Howell, W. S. (1977). Theoretical directions for intercultural communication. In M. K. Asante, E. Newmark, & C. Blake (Eds.), *Handbook of ethnomethodology.* Beverly Hills, CA: Sage.

Katz, R. L. (1963). *Empathy, its nature and uses.* London: Collier-Mac-Millan.

Keefe, T. (1976). Empathy: The critical skill. *Social Work, 21,* 10–14.

King, A.Y.C., & Bond, M. H. (1985). The Confucian paradigm of man: A sociological view. In W. S. Tseng & D.Y.H. Wu (Eds.), *Chinese culture and mental health* (pp. 29–42). Orlando, FL: Academic Press.

Kohut, H. (1966). Forms and transformation of narcissism. *Journal of the American Psychoanalytical Association, 14*, 243–272.

————. (1977). *The restoration of the self.* New York: International Universities Press.

Lambert, M. J., DeJulio, S. S., & Stein, D. M. (1978). Therapist interpersonal skills: Process, outcome, methodological considerations and recommendations for future research. *Psychological Bulletin, 85*, 467–489.

Lin, Y. S. (1974/1975). The evolution of the pre-Confucian meaning of Jen and Confucian concept of moral autonomy. *Monumenta Sinica, 31*, 172–204.

Mead, G. H. (1935). *Mind, self and society.* Chicago: University of Chicago.

Moore, C. A. (1967). Introduction: The humanistic Chinese mind. In C. A. Moore (Ed.), *The Chinese mind.* Honolulu: University of Hawaii Press.

Munakata, T. (1986). Socio-cultural factors of Japanese attitudes toward mental illness and mental health care delivery system. In D.Y. H. Wu & K. Sonoda (Eds.), *Proceedings for the Workshop on Modernization of East-Asian Medicine* (pp. 69–96), Tokyo, Dept. of Health Sociology, Tokyo University.

Neisser, J. (1976). *Cognition and reality.* New York: Freeman.

Rogers, C. R. (1951). *Client-centered therapy: Its current practice, implications, and theory.* Boston: Houghton-Mifflin.

————. (1957). The necessary and sufficient conditions of therapeutic personality change. *Journal of Consulting Psychology, 21*(2), 95–103.

————. (1975). Empathic: An unappreciated way of being. *The Counseling Psychologist, 5*(2), 2–10.

Sarbin, T R., & Allen, V. L. (1969). Role theory. In G. Lindzey & E. Aronson (Eds.), *The handbook of social psychology.* Reading, MA: Addison-Wesley.

Sue, S., & Zane, N. (1987). The role of culture and cultural techniques in psychotherapy. *American Psychologist, 42*(1), 37–45.

Truax, C. B., & Carkhuff, R. R. (1967). *Toward effective counseling and psychotherapy.* Chicago: Aldine.

White, G. M. (1982). The ethnographic study of culture knowledge of mental disorder. In G. M. White & A. J. Marsella (Eds.), *Cultural conceptions of mental health and therapy.* Boston, MA: D. Reidel.

White, G. M., & Marsella, A. J. (1982). Introduction: Cultural conceptions in mental health research and practice. In G. M. White & A. J. Marsella (Eds.), *Cultural conceptions of mental health and therapy.* Boston, MA: D. Reidel.

Wu, D.Y.H. (1987, August). *Achieving intra-cultural and inter-cultural understanding in psychotherapy with Asian Americans.* Paper presented at the Interactive Forum on Transference and Empathy in Psychotherapy with Asian Americans, South Cove Community Health Center and University of Massachusetts, Boston, MA.

Yamamoto, J. (1982). *Psychotherapy for Asian Americans.* Paper presented at the Second Pacific Congress of Psychiatry, Korea Extension Meeting, The Korean Neuropsychiatric Association, Seoul, Korea.

Yamamoto, J., & Chang, C. (1987, August). *Empathy for the family and the individual in the social context.* Paper presented at the Interactive Forum on Transference and Empathy in Psychotherapy with Asian Americans, South Cove Community Health Center and University of Massachusetts, Boston, MA.

Part II

Case Discussions

A Case of Biracial Identity Confusion

Gloria Chieko Saito

In her work with a 26-year-old American-born Chinese-Black male, Gloria Chieko Saito provided examples of both empathy and transference issues in psychotherapy with an ethnic minority client. Robert, whose mother is Chinese and whose father is Black, sought therapy because of conflicts that are, as David Wu would describe them, both intercultural and intracultural in nature. That is, the client's presenting problems included: feelings of confusion and disillusionment regarding his beliefs in Christianity, his problematic relationship with a Caucasian woman, his choice of graduate study in Chinese history and culture, and his feelings of rage toward his Black father, who had physically and emotionally abused him as a child. To know or understand the perspective of this client, who is described by Dr. Saito as growing up without roots in either the Asian or Black cultures, requires from the therapist both an empathic understanding of the client's affective perspective of his own inner world and an understanding of the social interaction. The stigma of a biracial marriage becomes for the child of such a marriage a "struggle" to find a group or community to which he himself can truly belong, an affective state that the client poignantly described through his characterization of himself as a "desert person" who is destined to wander forever without belonging anywhere.

Dr. Saito considers knowing the client, that is, "building rapport," to be the major task of treatment. The task of knowing the client became for the therapist the development of a trusting relationship. The transference of the client toward the therapist intensified, in this case as the client became more disclosing of his personal life and his affect, especially his anger and rage toward his father and his disappointment in his mother, who was unable to protect him from his father's abuse. Personal feelings about how good or bad he was and whether anyone who knew him could ever really like him became an important focus within the therapy. As the transference intensified during the early months, the client initially sought a hierarchical relationship with the therapist by asking Dr. Saito "for more direction and structure to the therapy. . . . Tell me what you think of me," the client insisted. However, as the therapy progressed the client exhibited an identification with the therapist and even expressed an interest in pursuing the same profession, clinical psychology. The hierarchical nature of the relationship between the client and therapist altered as the client revealed not only his cultural context but also his intrapsychic state of being and found himself accepted by the therapist.

Major Theoretical Orientation of Therapist: Psychodynamic.

Language Used by Therapist and Client: English.

PRESENTING PROBLEMS

The patient, Robert, describes feelings of confusion and disillusionment and reports difficulties with an intimate relationship. In addition, his behavior provides evidence of his unresolved feelings of rage.

HISTORY OF DEMOGRAPHIC DATA

Robert is a 26-year-old Chinese-Black male who is currently in a graduate master's program in East Asian studies. He lives in a studio in graduate student housing on campus and is supported by a teaching fellowship.

Robert expresses feelings of confusion and disillusionment regarding his religious beliefs. He became a Christian two years ago and has been a devout Baptist since that time. However, recently he has become disillusioned with fundamentalist theology and feels that the church is too rigid and does not allow for cultural differences among people. He is also disillusioned about his choice of graduate study. He has begun to feel that studying Chinese history and culture will not provide him with the sense of identification and belonging that he yearns for. He is having minor academic difficulties and procrastinates doing assignments.

Robert reports difficulties in his relationship of nine months with a Caucasian woman who is five years older. He feels distanced from her and has difficulty believing that she loves and cares for him. He ruminates about whether she is "right" for him and has excessive guilt about the fact that they have had premarital sex. Robert is also preoccupied with worries that he is sexually deviant. He is concerned that his sex drive is too strong and that he is committing sins against God by engaging in sexual activity and by being interested in pornography.

Robert is the fourth of five children born to a Chinese mother and a Black American father. He has three sisters and one brother. Robert was born in the United States and lived in San Francisco for most of his childhood. He reported being his mother's favorite child and was strongly influenced by her religious beliefs. She would force him to pray with her daily and constantly warned him that he would go to hell if he did not follow the ways of the Lord. The father was physically and emotionally abusive toward the mother and the children. Robert was beaten on numerous occasions and felt himself to be the scapegoat in his family. In addition, Robert's three sisters were sexually abused by the father. This abuse was never reported or confronted and has remained a family secret. The family had little connection with either the Chinese or Black communities in San Francisco. Robert grew up isolated from Asians and Blacks and felt that he was truly marginal and without roots in either culture.

At age 18, Robert went away to college and was heavily into using and dealing drugs. He was never caught or arrested for this activity, which stopped when he became a Baptist at age 24. He was also sexually promiscuous in college, engaging in brief, primarily sexual relationships with women. He had one long-term relationship with a woman in his senior year, which lasted until he graduated. In college, he had little sense of direction or purpose and finally graduated, after six years, with a degree in liberal arts. Upon graduation, Robert turned to Christianity in hopes of finding a meaningful direction for his life. He chose the Baptist church because he felt it would provide him with a structured set of rules by which he could live his life. At around the same time, he decided to pursue East Asian studies in order to explore his Chinese heritage and to feel more connected to the Asian part of his identity.

MENTAL STATUS AND CURRENT FUNCTIONING

At the time of the initial evaluation, Robert appeared to be mildly depressed and somewhat anxious. He was attractive, well-groomed, and appropriately dressed, with no abnormalities in behavior or speech. He was friendly, articulate, and able to express his thoughts in a clear and relevant manner. He appeared to be eager to share information during the interview but was embarrassed by the nature of his disclosures. He displayed a significant preoccupation with sexual issues, including guilt for his interest in pornography and for having had premarital sex. He also reported having minor difficulties with concentration on school work. He complained of his tendency to procrastinate and berated himself for cheating at times and for not being more organized and timely in his assignments. There was no evidence of perceptual disturbance or thought disorder. Memory, orientation, abstract thinking, insight, and judgment were all good. His attitude during the initial evaluation was open but somewhat distanced. It was clear that he had strong intellectual defenses but was experiencing sufficient emotional pain to be open to therapeutic intervention.

DIAGNOSTIC FORMULATION

Robert is a young man who was initially quite confused and disillusioned about a number of major aspects of his life. His choices of academic interest and religion appeared to be sincere but ineffective attempts to provide himself with a sense of identity and direction. From a cultural perspective, Robert found himself to be between two distinct and separate worlds and was struggling desperately to find a group or community to which he could truly belong. His history of abuse and family conflict and the cultural differences between his Chinese mother and his Black father appear to have contributed significantly to the sense of marginality that Robert so profoundly experienced. His difficulties with sexuality and moral values also appear to have their roots in the severe conflict and the physical, emotional, and sexual abuse within his family. Robert's primary defenses in dealing with these difficult conflicts were intellectualization and avoidance. In addition, he tended to ruminate about his difficulties and was plagued by preoccupations and doubt regarding his sexual, academic, and religious interests and his place in the Chinese and Black communities.

Based on these observations, Robert was given the following diagnosis:

Axis I: Obsessive compulsive disorder

                                     Identity disorder

Axis II: No diagnosis

TREATMENT PLAN

Robert has been seen in weekly individual psychotherapy for the past year for a total of 56 sessions. Short-term goals involved reducing his preoccupations regarding his sexual interests and helping him to clarify and understand the nature of his difficulties with his girlfriend. Long-term goals included helping him to resolve his feelings about his childhood abuse and helping him to come to terms with his family, particularly his fathers. In addition, resolving his religious conflicts, setting goals for future professional development, and coming to terms with issues of cultural and ethnic identity were important long-term goals.

SUMMARY OF TREATMENT

During the first two to three months of therapy, Robert was both eager and ambivalent about engaging in the therapeutic relationship. He brought up important issues around his childhood abuse and current difficulties with his girlfriend, Sherry, but tended to avoid important details and feelings. His approach to these problems was therefore highly intellectualized, and he appeared to be hiding important information about himself. One of the ways in which he did this was always to have a written agenda for the sessions. During our discussions, he would follow the agenda and then take careful notes. In fact, his wish to conceal information was quite explicit, as seen in the following excerpt from an early session.

> Robert: It feels funny to come in here and talk about all of this stuff. Like I know it's good for me, but it's hard at the same time.
>
> Therapist: That's understandable; you hardly know me.
>
> Robert: There are some things that I don't think I can ever tell you. . . .[pause] There are three experiences in my life—they all have to do with sex—that I can't talk about. I just don't feel comfortable letting you know about them.
>
> Therapist: It sounds like these experiences were quite difficult for you to deal with.
>
> Robert: They were, and if I told you, then you would think that there was something wrong with me.
>
> Therapist: You're really worried what I would think if you shared these things with me.
>
> Robert: Yes. That's why I can't, and won't share them with you.

During this initial phase of treatment, building rapport was a major task of the treatment. Robert related to me in a friendly and cordial manner, but he appeared to be distanced and constricted in sharing his feelings. During these sessions, Robert focused on sexual difficulties with Sherry, including the fact that his sex drive was very strong and felt insatiable at times. When Sherry was unwilling to respond to Robert's advances, he reported feeling rejected and vulnerable. He also expressed insecurities about himself and his identity as either an Asian or a Black and felt confused and constricted.

During the third month of treatment, Robert began to have recollections of being abused as a child. He expressed much anger and rage at his father and disappointment that his mother could not protect him from this abuse. At this point in treatment, he began to reveal the secret sexual experiences that he had previously kept from me.

Robert: I'm just so angry at my Dad—I can't see anything good about him. [pause] He would beat the shit out of me for no reason. The most horrible part [pauses, tearful] was that I always felt that there was something wrong with me because I was being beaten.

Therapist: Your father made you feel like it was all your fault instead of taking responsibility for his actions.

Robert: And my mother! She told me I was the cause of our family's problems, and that she wished I had never been born because then I wouldn't have had to be abused.

Therapist: You felt you couldn't count on the one person you thought you could rely on. Not only that, but it felt as though she betrayed you.

Robert: You know, more than anything, I'm furious at my Dad for sexually abusing my sisters. . . .[tearful] You know, one of those experiences I couldn't tell you about? I'm so ashamed [overcome with tears] . . . I had incest with my sister when I was eight or nine years old. I'm so ashamed.

Therapist: You really blame yourself for that.

Robert: I do. And I think it screwed her up, too. She's such an angry person now. And she has a hard time talking to me. It's really my fault.

Therapist: You blame yourself for all of the bad things that happened in your family. But can you see that your behavior was the result of how messed up your father and your mother were?

Robert: I guess so. But I still can't forgive myself.

Therapist: No matter how much you try to atone, or how good you try to be, you don't feel that you deserve to be forgiven or to be happy.

After this session, Robert began to ask me to give more direction and structure to the therapy sessions. He expressed the wish to be "cured" and stated that he was uncomfortable with the fluid nature of our conversations.

Robert: I would really like some feedback from you sometimes. I feel like I talk a lot about what's happening with me, and you sit there and don't say anything. Can't you tell me how I can feel better? I'd like for you to tell me what to talk about here. Maybe then we'd make some progress.

Therapist: You really want me to fix things up so that you don't experience any more pain or conflict or confusion. I wish that working out this stuff was that easy, but it's not. It's like you expect me to have some magic formula to fix you up, and you're really disappointed and angry that I don't.

Robert: I'm not angry at you. I just don't think I'm making any progress here.

Therapist: Let's talk about progress. What does that mean to you?

Robert: I'd like to feel better—to be more centered and secure—to feel like I'm ok. But how do I go about doing that?

Therapist: Well, it seems that it would be important for us to identify clearly some of the problems and goals that we can work on together. We've talked about some of this before, but maybe it would help to discuss it again.

Robert: But how can I trust that you can really help me? I feel like I've really exposed myself to you and that I'm leaving myself open to you. I don't know if I want to do that.

Therapist: You're having difficulty in trusting me, and you're feeling really vulnerable because now I have all of this information about you. The issue of trust is a big thing for you.

During the following months, Robert dealt with his feelings of being an outsider, destined to struggle with issues of racial oppression. He characterized himself as a "desert person" who had to wander forever, without the comforts of belonging to any village or having any permanent home. The symbolism was quite striking, and Robert was able to relate this to his intense feelings of being marginal and unacceptable to any racial group because of his mixed Chinese-Black heritage. He also struggled with the issue of whether or not to remain in the Baptist church. He attributed some of his difficulties with his girlfriend Sherry to the fact that she is Caucasian, has a clear sense of who she is and where she belongs, and has never had to struggle with issues of abuse, minority status, or severe family conflict. He expressed ambivalence about the direction of their relationship and alternated between wanting to marry her, feeling envious of and inferior to her, and wanting to separate from her. He also expressed much discomfort with his feelings of dependence on Sherry, as well as fear of becoming more involved and emotionally intimate. After several months of struggling with these issues, they decided to end the relationship. Robert felt intensely betrayed and rejected by Sherry, despite the fact that this was a mutual decision.

At this point in the therapy, Robert again expressed the need for feedback from me, as well as feelings of anger about the slow progress of treatment.

Robert: I really feel better, but it seems like it takes forever. I wish it would go faster, and that it wouldn't be so hard. I also wish you'd tell me what you think of me.

Therapist: What is it that you're asking of me?

Robert: Well, I guess I wonder if you think I'm crazy or worthless.

Therapist: Is there anything I do that makes you feel that way?

Robert: Well, sometimes I feel like you think I'm an interesting case, and that you talk to others about me, and that you don't really care. After all, it's just a job to you, but it's my life to me.

Therapist: Why would I do something like that?

Robert: I don't know. It's just the way I feel.

Therapist: I have the sense that you're feeling quite vulnerable right now, and you're wondering whom you can trust, and what you can count on in your life. You trusted Sherry, and you feel she rejected you. Maybe you're afraid that if you trust me, I'll do the same thing.

Robert: That's true. Why do I do that? I always seem to mess myself up.

Therapist: It's hard for you to just accept your feelings without dumping on yourself for them. It's as though if you have a feeling that's uncomfortable or difficult, there's something wrong with you. And if you feel there's something wrong with you, you're afraid that you'll be rejected, too.

Subsequent to this session, Robert began to express more of his need and dependence on me as the therapist. He has been able to acknowledge that no matter how much, that it is not enough. At the end of one of these discussions, Robert had difficulty leaving the session, stating, "I don't want to go, and why do I have to leave anyway?"

The issue of "not enough" has continued to be prominent in the sessions. Robert has expressed the feeling that perhaps a therapist who had personal experience with physical and sexual abuse would be better able to help him work through his conflicts in this area. Exploration and confrontation by me of his needs and feelings of being odd or damaged because of his experiences has helped me to move beyond the anger and to further develop the therapeutic alliance.

Recently, Robert has exhibited an increased need for validation from me and an identification with me. He has expressed an interest in becoming a clinical psychologist and has questioned me at length about whether or not this would be a good idea. Exploration of the issues has helped Robert to clarify his own motivations for entering the field. The following is an excerpt from a recent sessions.

Robert: I wondered what you thought about my going into clinical psychology. Do you think it's good idea?

Therapist: You seem to want me to tell you that I approve of this choice.

Robert: I think it would be a good field for me. I think I'm sensitive to people, and very caring, and that I could be good at it. But I also worry about whether I'm interested in it for the wrong reasons.

Therapist: What do you mean?

Robert: Well, I'm interested in studying it to learn more about how therapy works. I know what it feels like to be in it, and I know that I feel better, but I really don't understand how it works. I think it would be good for me to get a handle on it academically.

Therapist: So you're interested in the field sort of as a way to heal yourself, to feel like you understand what's happening to you as you experience the changes in yourself.

Robert: That's right. But, God, what would my mother say!

Therapist: She wouldn't approve?

Robert: She would say that religion is the only answer; that psychology is the "Devil's work." [laughs]

Therapist: You're quite concerned about what your mother would think about this, and you're also concerned about what I would think, whether or not I would approve.

Robert: That's true, it is important. I'm afraid that you think it's a crazy idea.

CURRENT STATUS OF CASE

Robert has progressed considerably in the past year of therapy. His obsessional thoughts about his sexuality have decreased, and he appears to be less concerned that he is a sexual deviant for his interests in pornography. His preoccupations with his sexual drive have decreased, and he is more concerned with taking care of himself physically and emotionally. Robert has also taken significant steps toward resolving the anger, guilt, and negative self-evaluations that stem from his childhood abuse and severe family conflict. He is able to express more directly his anger toward both his parents and has begun to see the profound deficits in their ability to care for themselves, much less for their children. He has even taken steps toward identifying and integrating some of the positive aspects of his father's character and plans to write a story about his father's migration to the Bay Area from the Deep South.

CONCLUDING STATEMENT

Robert's therapy has focused largely on clarifying, understanding, and interpreting his reactions to, and demands of, the therapist. At times it has involved sharing the therapist's reactions in a direct way with him. Robert has responded to confrontation and clarification in a positive way, and this has served to deepen the therapeutic alliance and further therapeutic progress.

DISCUSSIONS QUESTIONS

1. It was very important in this case for the therapist to examine her own feelings about the biracial background of the client. Where can a therapist turn to find support for, and opportunities to engage constructively in, such self-examination?

2. Therapy by its very nature focuses inward. Does a mixed-race client such as this one also need opportunities to focus his energies externally on the treatment of biracial individuals by others? How important is it for the therapy to go on in a context where the individual is being helped to change himself in order to bring about social change more effectively?

3. How important was it to this client to have an Asian therapist in working through identity issues and feelings of marginality?

4. Given the client's issues with sexuality, how might the fact that the therapist is female contribute to the transference relationship?

5

Synthesizing Eastern and Western Psychotherapeutic Approaches

George K. Hong

This case of a 52-year-old Chinese immigrant who has been in the United States for approximately 20 years illustrates the strong tendency of Asian clients to experience psychological distress somatically. Mr. Chan had been referred for psychotherapy by his physician, who could find no medical basis for his frequent chest pains and persistent fears about having a heart attack. Mr. Chan was initially preoccupied with his health concerns and was eager to prove that his complaints had a legitimate biological basis. When Western medicine did not confirm his somatic complaints, he became skeptical about its value and effectiveness.

The case material provides an opportunity to examine the ways in which racial/ethnic transference and active empathy are manifested in psychotherapy with a therapist and client who share the same cultural heritage. In spite of the match between the race and ethnicity of the therapist and client, the client still engaged initially in testing the therapist's knowledge about and acceptance of his cultural heritage. It appears to be the integration of Chinese cultural concepts into "Western" psychotherapy that finally established a positive therapeutic alliance and allowed the client to accept the therapist's interventions. In order to engage the client and to ensure compliance, the therapist chose to take on an authoritative role as in the traditional doctor-patient and teacher-student relationships. It should be noted that his hierarchical relationship was authoritative but not authoritarian in nature. The therapist based his authority on his expert knowledge, which was in keeping with the expectations of the client. Throughout the treatment, the therapist remained respectful of the client's questions and suggestions and attempted to integrate them with his own therapeutic suggestions.

This case also highlights the concept of active empathy, discussed in Part I. The therapist went beyond merely communicating his understanding of the client's problems and feelings and took an active role in helping the client address key issues. The therapist not only let the client know that he understood and cared, but also showed that he cared enough to help the client do something instrumental about his problems. Empathy in this case also involved recognizing the client's limits and working at his pace, knowing what issues to explore first and what issues to leave for later, knowing whether to approach an issue directly or indirectly, and making appropriate judgments about the client's degree of acculturation and the relevance of cultural issues to both problem definition and treatment.

Major Theoretical Orientation of Therapist: Cognitive behavioral.

Language Used by Therapist and Client: Chinese (Cantonese), the client's primary language.

PRESENTING PROBLEMS

Mr. Chan has frequent somatic compliants, especially chest pains, and is particularly concerned about having heart attacks. He also exhibits symptoms of anxiety. He was referred by his physician after physical causes had been ruled out.

HISTORY AND DEMOGRAPHIC DATA

Mr. Chan is a Chinese immigrant living with his wife and three teenage daughters. He speaks some English, but his dominant language is Chinese. At the time of intake, he and his wife were 52 and 38 years old respectively.

Mr. Chan was born and reared in China. He is the only child in his family. After completing junior high school, he helped with his parents' small business. A few years after the Communist takeover, he left his parents to go to Hong Kong. He was then in his early twenties. He lived in Hong Kong for a few years and in another Southeast Asian country for another few years. In both places, he worked at low-level jobs for relatives and attended some evening or part-time school. He had some college classes.

At age 31, Mr. Chan came to the United States and worked as a cook in Chinese restaurants. About five years later, he returned to Hong Kong and, through an arrangement made by friends, got married. The couple returned to the United States. Their children were born in this country. They were doing well in school. Mrs. Chan worked as a seamstress in the garment factories. Mr. Chan continued to work as a cook until about seven years ago, when he changed occupations to become a cashier for a major company. The reason for the change was mainly job security and better financial and fringe benefits.

FUNCTIONING AT TIME OF EVALUATION

Mr. Chan was appropriately dressed. He was cooperative and verbal. He was eager to justify his somatic complaints and health concerns. He related that in the past three years, he had a lot of medical problems. These included a sinus problem that was not properly identified for a long time even after he was examined by a number of specialists. Eventually, it was corrected through a minor operation. He also had problems with his teeth, gallbladder stones, varicose veins, and a sprained ankle. Currently, he was preoccupied with his health. He was extremely sensitive to any discomfort he felt and had presented numerous somatic complaints to his physicians. He was particularly concerned about having cardiovascular problems and frequently complained of chest pains, heart palpitations, and shoulder pains. He often interpreted these symptoms as heart attacks and panicked. On a few occasions, he called his physicians for emergency help in the middle of the night.

Once, he had to be taken away from work in an ambulance for what he falsely reported as a heart attack. He took frequent sick leaves to consult physicians and recently received a reprimand from his company for doing so. He also reported frequent nightmares that woke him up in the middle of the night. Most of these involved dreams of getting lost. Medical checkups indicated no basis for his chest pains, shoulder pains, and other physical complaints. He was prescribed Xanax, an anti-anxiety medication, by one of his physicians. However, his complaints continued, and he also went to different physicians for examinations. Consequently, he was referred for psychotherapy.

Mr. Chan was alert, oriented, with intact memory and no sign of psychotic disorders. He admitted to his sensitivity about his health. He was aware of his physicians' skepticism regarding his complaints. He kept detailed written accounts of his illnesses and medical treatments and went through these with me to prove that his health concerns were valid. Discussion of daily activities revealed that he was organizing his life around his symptoms. For example, in order to avoid the nightmares, he slept on a sofa in the living room instead of his bed. He believed that it was less comfortable and he would have fewer dreams. He followed a rigid and orderly daily routine and prepared "health foods" and herbal soups to "strengthen" his body in the traditional Chinese medical concept of "Po" (phonetic translation from Cantonese). He also took walks and tried exercises such as Tai-Chi as part of his body-strengthening regimen. He read extensively about medical issues in Chinese books and magazines.

Besides his preoccupation with health, Mr. Chan's daily functioning was within normal limits. He performed his share of household chores and maintained an active social relationship with friends. While he admitted that Mrs. Chan and the children frowned on his concerns about health and his rigid daily routines, he indicated that they were used to them. Furthermore, because of his work schedule, he did not have much common time with his family. He worked afternoon and night shifts with a weekday as his day off, while Mrs. Chan worked from early morning to evening and had the weekends off. The children were in school and had their own circle of friends. Thus, Mr. Chan's routine did not bother them too much. At work, with the exception of his frequent sick leaves, he had no problems in performing his duties.

DIAGNOSTIC FORMULATION

The dominant problem exhibited by Mr. Chan was his preoccupation with his health, especially the belief that he might have a serious illness. He was overly sensitive to physical sensations and tended to exaggerate them. He often interpreted them as signs of a major disease, especially of an impending heart attack. Although he verbally agreed with his physicians that he was physically healthy, he continued to behave as if he were weak and vulnerable. He organized his life around his health concerns and tried hard to "strengthen" himself. His frequent sick leaves were affecting his record at work, and his false heart attack that necessitated calling in an ambulance was certainly disruptive. Although his complaints went beyond those of cardiovascular problems, he did not have a sufficient number of symptoms to meet the criteria of somatization disorder. Also, his preoccupation about having a disease, particularly heart disease, was the dominant clinical feature. Thus, a diagnosis of hypochondriasis was indicated.

Mr. Chan also demonstrated some symptoms of anxiety and panic disorders. However, the frequency of his panic behavior did not meet the criteria of panic disorder. Furthermore, his anxiety appeared to be focused on health concerns. Often, it seemed to interact with his faulty interpretation of his physical sensations, and they escalated in a vicious cycle that further convinced him that he was really having a heart attack and caused him to panic. Thus, although anxiety and panic disorders were originally considered as possible diagnoses, they were eventually ruled out as the predominance of his concern about physical health emerged more clearly during the initial stage of therapy.

He was given the following DSM III diagnosis:

Axis I: 300.70 Hypochondriasis
Axis II: No diagnosis

TREATMENT PLAN

Treatment goals were: (1) to help Mr. Chan lower his anxiety concerning his physical health; (2) to help him develop ways of coping with his anxiety, including relaxation training; (3) to help him develop insight regarding his fears and concerns about having a serious illness; and (4) to monitor and gradually eliminate his dependence on medication.

For the first six months, Mr. Chan was seen weekly for psychotherapy. He was also seen by a psychiatrist, Dr. Bom Sang Lee, who monitored his medication. The medication visits averaged about once a month. Dr. Lee and I maintained close contact and worked as a team. Then, Mr. Chan having made satisfactory progress, psychotherapy was reduced to once every two weeks for the next ten months. Termination was achieved after five more monthly sessions.

SUMMARY OF SESSIONS AND TREATMENT

In the beginning, a major portion of time during the sessions was spent in reviewing Mr. Chan's medical history. His family situation was discussed, but his assertion that he had no family problems was respected and this issue was not brought up until a later time. I accepted Mr. Chan's presentation of his previous medical problems but emphasized that such problems had probably overly sensitized him about health issues. The differences between reasonable sensitivity versus oversensitivity and the need to label his somatic experiences appropriately and to redirect his attention from major illnesses were discussed. Deep-muscle relaxation was introduced during the third session. Subsequent sessions gradually included meditation and relaxation imagery through informal hypnotic-trance induction. The first psychiatric appointment to discuss his use of Xanax was held after the seventh session.

The problems of drug dependency were explained then, and he accepted the advice to taper off medication in favor of psychotherapy.

During this initial period, my main objective was to engage Mr. Chan in psychotherapy. This was done through an attempt to empathically understand Mr. Chan's subjective perception of the situation. It was noted that Mr. Chan did not see his problems as psychological. He also did not have any idea of how psychotherapy would work. He came at the recommendation of his physicians, seeking a quick cure for his problems. He was eager to prove that he was not "crazy" and produced the written record of his past illnesses, especially his misdiagnosed sinus problem, to assert that he had a rational basis for his complaints. I did not challenge his perception. The large portion of time spent in reviewing medical history conveyed to Mr. Chan that his complaints were taken seriously. It also gave him the chance to express his frustration and anxiety.

Acknowledging his eagerness for a firm answer, I as the psychologist, in a rather authoritative manner, defined his problem as oversensitivity to health caused by past medical issues. Recognizing his desire for a quick cure, I introduced relaxation exercises early in the therapy to give him a means of coping with his anxiety. In spite of his skepticism, Mr. Chan followed his physician's advice to come for psychotherapy. I had to rely on this perceived authority of the physician to engage Mr. Chan. Any disagreement between psychologist and physician would cause more confusion for him. Thus although I did not believe that Xanax would be helpful, I did not bring up the issue until a firmer therapeutic relationship had been established. Also, by that time, Mr. Chan had already been practicing relaxation exercises for a few weeks and reporting success. This made it easier to convince him that there were other ways besides medication to address his problems.

I always tried to use concepts and terms that were familiar to Mr. Chan. Much effort was spent in helping him understand the relationship between psychological and somatic experiences. For example, in the initial sessions, Mr. Chan would typically begin by bringing up his medical history and somatic complaints. I would let him repeat these issues but guided the discussion by asking for further clarification of specific incidents. This gave me an opportunity to discuss the anxiety Mr. Chan experienced during his perceived "heart attacks," and how anxiety would result in physiological changes that could further escalate his "heart attack" symptoms. Anxiety was discussed using various Chinese terms, such as "tenseness" or "excited" ("kan cheung" in Cantonese) and "fearful" ("gang" in Cantonese). The first term was used more often as Mr. Chan seemed to see "fearful" as having somewhat judgmental or scornful connotations. The relationship between anxiety, stress, and cardiovascular problems was discussed, to help him to see the relationship between psychological and physical problems. Then the relaxation exercises were introduced as a means for him to control his anxiety symptoms. The benefits of relaxation exercises in reducing stress-related problems were also discussed. Thus he also perceived the exercises to be a way of preventing cardiovascular problems and was even more receptive to them. Deep-muscle relaxation was chosen specifically because it involved moving various muscle groups, and this could reinforce the idea of the relationship between "body" and "mind." I gave specific instructions on when to perform the exercise, such as, once in the morning between breakfast and lunch, once before bedtime, and an abbreviated exercise whenever he felt anxious. Such prescription-like instructions appealed to Mr. Chan's familiarity with the medical model and helped to ensure confidence and compliance. In subsequent sessions, relaxation imageries, such as walking on a beach or meadow, were introduced through indirect trance induction. Gradually, Mr. Chan was able to achieve relaxation through these imageries rather than going through the exercise.

The connection between stress, anxiety, and somatic symptoms was further reviewed in each session, giving me a smooth transition into a discussion of Mr. Chan's daily activities as well as work and home environment, exploring emotional issues that might be related to his preoccupation with health. Discussion of daily activities also led smoothly into a discussion of relationships with family members. I was cautious in discussing these issues, often prefacing questions to reflect an interest in the relationship between the family situation and his problems, rather than an interest in family relationships per se, which might be considered too intrusive. For example, I would say, "Mr. Chan, you seem to be so busy all the time. This really builds up a lot of tension. Do you have any leisure activities such as going out with your family?" It was only at the fifth session that a more detailed discussion of family life was initiated. Gradually, these discussions revealed stresses at work and at home that needed to be addressed.

Mr. Chan seemed to pride himself in being a self-educated man, in the sense that since junior high school, he had to struggle with work and part-time school. He presented himself in an educated manner, often quoting Chinese proverbs or classics in his conversations. He also frequently used traditional Chinese medical concepts in discussing health issues. His manner of speech and frequent mention of Chinese medicine reflected a certain skepticism toward Western medicine, with the implication that his physicians might be missing something. Furthermore, these were likely to be attempts to find out whether I was "just" another "Western" professional who would never fully understand his problems.

I met his challenge by discussing these Chinese medical concepts with him and not disapproving of his use of herbal soups or health foods to "strengthen" his body. In fact I appealed to his knowledge of Chinese health issues and helped him to integrate them with psychotherapy. For example, while learning relaxation exercises and trance imageries, Mr. Chan raised the question of their similarities with the traditional practices of meditation, Tai-Chi, and Chi-Kung, many of which he had tried before. I discussed these issues by asking him to describe his subjective experience regarding the similarity between them. I frankly stated that although I knew the general principles of these practices, they were beyond my specialization and I would like him to focus on relaxation techniques. He could try these other practices as long as he found them helpful, but he was not to mix them together with the relaxation exercises. This provided a balance between cultural practices and psychotherapeutic techniques. I used quotations only sparingly in conversations, as this was his own style of talking. I did it once in a while, just to demonstrate my familiarity with Chinese culture or just to get a point across. This was done in a natural, noncompetitive manner. Mr. Chan was very responsive to such an approach.

At one point, I tried to explain to Mr. Chan the need to put things in proper perspective and not to overreact to events. Mr. Chan seemed to have difficulty understanding or accepting this concept. I did some preparation before the next session and then illustrated this concept to him by quoting the Confucian classic "Doctrine of *Chung Yung"* ("Doctrine of the Mean or Middle.") The exchange went approximately like this:

> Psychologist: Mr. Chan, you seem to have read a lot of the classics. I wonder whether you remember what the "Doctrine of *Chung Yung"* says?
>
> Mr. Chan: I am not sure . . .
>
> Psychologist: The passage is " . . . *Chung* is when there is no arousal of feelings of pleasure, anger, sorrows or joy; *Yung* is when these feelings are aroused and they are in the appropriate degree. . . ." [This is an abbreviation of the actual passage quoted, since the translation is quite cumbersome.]

I then proceeded to discuss the concept. Ths exchange reported here was of particular significance. About a year later, at the termination session, Mr. Chan took a slip of paper from his pocket and showed it to me. The quotation was written on it. He reiterated that he found it to be really meaningful and helpful and that he would always remember it.

The transference process in this case was clearly facilitated by the common cultural background of the psychologist and client. It should be noted that it was not just the external appearance but rather the psychologist's ability to appropriately apply culturally relevant knowledge that made the difference. The therapeutic alliance was not firmly established until the client had "tested" the psychologist's understanding and acceptance of his cultural and philosophical background. Through this process of testing, he eventually viewed the psychologist as an authority who could treat him, as well as a mentor who could help him reorganize his daily life and redirect his concerns from his health to other more appropriate issues.

After Mr. Chan was given enough time to become more comfortable in discussing family issues, his wife was invited to come in so they could participate as a couple for a session. This was at the thirteenth session. Both of them complained about stress at work and admitted to frequent bickering at home. Mrs. Chan expressed frustration and annoyance at Mr. Chan's oversensitivity and "constant nagging" about health and safety, while Mr. Chan expressed dissatisfaction about her lack of respect for his experience as well as lack of appreciation of his concern for her. It was apparent that Mr. Chan had a paternalistic attitude toward her. After this evaluative session, no further couple sessions were held. I was aware of Mr. Chan's desire not to show his weaknesses in front of his wife and of his conviction that he could deal with his problems by himself. The children were not invited to any session, as it would be perceived as an even greater threat to Mr. Chan's dignity as the head of the household.

While I respected Mr. Chan's limits, I continued to address family issues in individual sessions. There, Mr. Chan was more open and willing to admit his role in causing tensions at home. I eventually helped him to recognize his overprotectiveness and to take a more relaxed attitude at home. It is of interest to note that Mr. Chan's health preoccupation might possibly be related to his overprotectiveness, such as an underlying fear that his family would be helpless if he were to die or a need to use the somatic symptoms as a reminder that he still had responsibilities to fulfill and could not die yet—an even more paradoxical insecurity in the face of the growing independence of his children and wife. I did not confront him with these issues. Rather, I discussed them indirectly and helped Mr. Chan to realize that although his family was not totally dependent on him, he still had an important role in it. I also helped him to redirect his attention and energy to developing his leisure activities, such as taking adult education courses, which he eventually did with expressed satisfaction.

In the area of medication, I was present at many of the sessions with Dr. Lee. This helped to reduce the confusion often caused by having a client seen by different providers. The united front presented by psychologist and psychiatrist also helped to reassure the client that there was no "lost communication" between providers. Such close coordination between providers is particularly important for clients who are not familiar with mental health services and often feel perplexed by the roles of different providers.

About a month after the first medication visit, Mr. Chan, in his eagerness to taper off Xanax, stopped taking it completely in a short period of time. He developed severe rebound effects. Recognizing the serious addictive nature of Xanax, he became even more determined not to take it. Tofranil was prescribed as an alternative. However, he reacted negatively to its side effects and reluctantly went back to Xanax. In both incidents, Mr. Chan repeatedly expressed his distress in subsequent psychotherapy sessions and, in his typical manner, exaggerated his physical reactions at each recounting of the experiences. Rather than confronting him, I used these occasions as opportunities to illustrate to him that physical symptoms were not necessarily life-threatening and, in fact, that his physical distress in both cases was predictable and easily reversible. This further helped him to recognize his tendency to interpret every somatic discomfort as the sign of a fatal illness.

The foundations of therapy were firmly laid after the first six months. By this time, Mr. Chan had accepted the psychological basis of his problems. He realized that he was overly sensitive about illnesses. He was more aware of the causal relationship between his anxiety and "heart attack" symptoms. He still complained of chest and shoulder pains and various other symptoms, but he no longer panicked. He began to attribute the pains to less life-threatening problems, such as rheumatism. He was able to stay through his shift at work despite the symptoms and found the relaxation techniques helpful. Since the initiation of therapy, he no longer made frantic phone calls to his physicians for help. His nightmares had also diminished. His dosage of Xanax had been reduced. Given the amount of progress, sessions were reduced to every two weeks. This gave Mr. Chan a confirmation of his achievement and helped to maintain his motivation in therapy.

During the next ten months, I continued to help Mr. Chan gain further insights regarding his preoccupation with health and to help him deal with the stress he experienced at home and at work. His expectations for himself and his family members, as well as his attitude toward them, were discussed. In the sessions, specific incidents that happened during the past two weeks and the ways he handled them were often reviewed. Daily routines were examined and reorganized. His preoccupation with illnesses was redirected to more appropriate activities, such as leisure walks, Tai-Chi, and relaxation exercises. The focus in this period was to consolidate the therapeutic gains and help Mr. Chan apply the principles he had learned previously. He was also helped to further reduce his dosage of Xanax. Given his earlier negative experience in tapering off his dosage too quickly, Mr. Chan was taking a much more cautious and slower approach now.

After ten months of biweekly sessions, Mr. Chan had achieved most of the therapeutic goals and was able to maintain his progress. He reported that he was no longer preoccupied with illnesses. When he experienced occasional somatic discomforts, he was able to put them into proper perspective without feeling alarmed. He had taken steps to reduce his bickering with Mrs. Chan and reported the family situation to be more satisfying. His nightmares had stopped. He no longer slept on the sofa and had moved back into the bedroom. At this time, he was on a minimal dosage of Xanax (1/4 of a 0.25-mg pill per day, as compared to 10 mg per day in the beginning). However, he was apprehensive about stopping it for fear of rebound effects. In the next five months, sessions were reduced to monthly. His dosage was reduced further, and he eventually stopped taking Xanax. During this period, I also reviewed the therapeutic progress with Mr. Chan and reinforced the therapeutic concepts. Treatment was then successfully terminated.

CONCLUDING STATEMENT

This case illustrates a number of issues in psychotherapy with Chinese Americans. Some of these are rather general, such as the need to educate the client regarding the nature of psychological problems and psychotherapy, having some knowledge of traditional Chinese medical concepts and Chinese philosophy, knowing which topics might be considered intrusive, and respecting the family hierarchy. They are probably applicable to many cases. Other techniques used here, such as using quotations to illustrate therapeutic concepts, are more specific to this case. Their application to other cases has to be selective. The basic principle I follow is to work at the client's level, applying cultural concepts as needed, without stereotyping or using those concepts to excess.

DISCUSSION QUESTIONS

1. At what point, if any, does it become necessary to examine directly the hierarchical transference relationship? Is it necessary to transcend the hierarchical transference or is it, given the client's strongly held cultural beliefs about the authority of the doctor, simply a means to a positive therapeutic outcome?

2. How does the manifestation of somatic symptoms reflect the cultural views of this client?

3. How does the therapist use his understanding of the client's symptoms to develop a therapeutic alliance and enhance the therapeutic process?

4. How has the use both of *predictive* empathy (a cognitive understanding of Asian culture) and of *active* empathy (the communication of empathy) been important to the outcome of this case?

5. What methods has the therapist used to reassure his client that he, the therapist, understands his client's reality?

6

A Case of Somatic Delusions

Siu Ping Ma

The following case of a 17-year-old Chinese male illustrates how the stresses of immigration and racial discrimination can interact with developmental issues (in this instance, adolescent identity confusion) to produce social isolation, paranoid delusions, and suicidal behavior.

The immigration of the patient and his family from Hong Kong three years earlier was disruptive for the family in a number of ways. In addition to being isolated from their extended family and having debts from the immigration expenses, the family now had to cope with the father's work-related absence (the father works in another town and returns home only once every one or two weeks). Moreover, the parents' competence and authority were decreased because of their dependence on the children to speak English. The patient, a physically underdeveloped adolescent, confronted racial discrimination in his school, where he was teased and even physically attacked because of his ethnicity. These social conditions exacerbated existing tension between the patient's parents and made more acute the mother's tendency to alternate between being emotionally overinvolved with the patient and punitive toward him.

These stressful experiences provide the backdrop against which to understand the patient's anxiety about his physical bodily changes and his ambivalence about his close dependent relationship with his mother and older sisters. The patient is described as having a "fragile sexual identity" and a "confused racial identity" manifested in his somatic delusions, which include the beliefs that his nose is growing larger and that he has an ugly skin disease that is causing people to shun him.

The case provides an excellent illustration of the concept of hierarchical transference. The therapist's being Chinese facilitated a contract with this severely disturbed adolescent to actively participate in treatment and to commit to not killing himself. This was accomplished by taking advantage of the respect accorded to doctors in Chinese society and the emphasis within the culture on compliance with authority. The case also illustrates the fragility of a hierarchical transference where the patient daily, even during treatment, experiences the clash of cultures. The patient's two hospitalizations brought this clash to the fore when the Chinese mental health team differed with the Western team about appropriate treatment, thereby calling into question the absolute authority of the Chinese mental health team. This resulted in the patient's disillusionment with treatment. His desire for an absolute authority had been challenged; he withdrew from treatment and took refuge in religion.

> *Major Theoretical Orientation of Therapist*: The orientation used in this case is eclectic with an emphasis on psychodynamic, systems, and psychosocial/educational approaches.

> *Language Used by Therapist and Client*: Chinese (Cantonese, the native dialect of the patient).

PRESENTING PROBLEM

Kai-Ming, a 17-year-old Chinese immigrant, was referred by a state outpatient agency for treatment of his paranoid delusions, suicidal ideation, and social isolation. He resisted treatment at the referring agency. He had been very anxious for the last year and a half because of delusions that his nose was becoming larger, his eyebrows were growing upward, and his facial skin was itching and peeling off. He believed that he was becoming ugly and that his "skin disease" was contagious. He believed that others disliked and shunned him. In desperation, he contemplated suicide. He thought that he should kill himself if he could not be cured. The family reported that recently Kai-Ming had been accumulating sleeping pills and playing with a razor. He displayed temper tantrums (crushing oranges, smashing rice bowls, banging the walls), and once, he even struck his father. Kai-Ming also exhibited bizarre behavior such as staring into the mirror excessively throughout the day.

The family reported that the problems began two years before, the second year after Kai-Ming's immigration to the United States. At that time his grades in school began to drop, and he was frequently truant. A few months later, he isolated himself completely, remaining in his house except to visit dermatologists. He also withdrew from interaction with the family for about the last seven months. Subsequently, he attempted suicide by cutting his wrist. He saved his blood in a glass, mixed it with water, and gave it to his mother.

FAMILY HISTORY AND DEMOGRAPHIC DATA

Kai-Ming was born in Hong Kong. He immigrated to the United States with his family three years ago. At the time of referral, he resided with both parents and three siblings. His father was 55 years old, and his mother was 50. Both were born in China and married in Hong Kong. Kai-Ming has four older sisters (ages ranging from 18 to 25) and one younger brother (age 16). The two oldest sisters are married and are still in Hong Kong. Kai-Ming has no extended family in the United States. His father works in an out-of-town Chinese restaurant and comes home only once every one or two weeks. His mother works in a garment factory in Chinatown six days a week for 11 to 12 hours a day. The patient and siblings help the mother in the factory after school from 7 to 9 P.M. The two youngest sisters attend college and are above-average students. The younger brother is attending high school.

Although the family was still in debt for the immigration expenses, they were not entitled to welfare. Benefits or financial aid were withheld because the two sisters in Hong Kong had set aside money in an account for their parents.

The parents were monolingual in Chinese, and their activities were limited to Chinatown because of the language and cultural barriers. They were dependent on the two daughters for translation and negotiation. They also relied on the daughters to take care of and to discipline the younger siblings.

There were only a small number of Asian students in Kai-Ming's school. He was frequently teased, called names, and even physically attacked at times because of his ethnicity.

FUNCTIONING AT TIME OF EVALUATION

Kai-Ming was an average student and had an adequate social life in Hong Kong before immigration. In the first year after immigration, he received an award for academic achievement. In the following year, he began to feel bad about himself and became withdrawn. He began to be truant and eventually dropped out of school and quit his part-time factory job. In the past year, he had become withdrawn and isolated. He would only go out occasionally to see medical doctors for treatment of problems relating to his somatic delusions. He resisted psychiatric services and did not comply with medication instructions.

Kai-Ming maintains minimum functioning at home. His major activities at home are watching television, listening to the radio, watching the water tap run, and staring into the mirror. He manages his personal hygiene and grooming.

MENTAL STATUS AT TIME OF EVALUATION

Kai-Ming was a 17-year-old physically underdeveloped Chinese male adolescent. He looked a few years younger than his age. He was alert and oriented. His speech was goal-oriented. When talked to about his suicidal ideation, he was indifferent. He denied any hallucination. He had ideas of reference and a somatic delusion. His concentration and memory were fair and judgment poor. His insight was poor.

DIAGNOSTIC FORMULATION

One year after immigration, Kai-Ming began to experience somatic delusions. The family history seemed uneventful. There is little information to explain the onset of the presenting problems.

The patient's symptoms may be understood in the following ways. The onset of his illness was precipitated by the psychosocial stressors from immigration. The fragmentation and disruption of the family structure exacerbated his already fragile sexual identity. This coupled with racial-identity issues brought upon by his immigration to the United States resulted in a breakdown of ego functions. His somatic delusion appears to be related to early ego pathology as well as to his current sexual and racial identity crisis. His delusion of a growing nose can be seen as symbolizing a number of conflicts, including his sexuality, growing independence, and the conflicts of his racial identity, as well as rationalization for racial discrimination. He revealed great ambivalence about growing up and gaining independence. He wished to have a child's face and a man's body. He wanted to grow up, and yet he did not want to. He also revealed his ambivalence in his racial image. He believed that the white American is good-looking with a "tall and narrow" nose and well-built, muscular body.

He also thought that blonde was beautiful. He wanted to look like the white Americans. However, he complained of his growing nose that made him ugly and disliked. At times, he wished his nose would grow back to its original size or smaller. He also wished at times to be "yellower." He became very ambivalent and self-conscious.

Kai-Ming's delusion of peeling facial skin and "sticking-up" eyebrows were also part of his obsession with his physical appearance and his paranoia. He believed that people would dislike him because of his funny, ugly look and his contagious skin disease. His family was very close-knit. The family structure followed the traditional Chinese vertical hierarchy, excluding the father, who lost his position and visibility in the family after immigration to the United States. His physical absence because of his work further removed him from a dominant role. He was seen as a weak character and was not respected by the family. The mother was dominant and powerful. She belittled the father. However, she did not allow the children to demean him and would use him as a figure-head in important matters or decisions. After the first and second oldest sisters got married, the third and fourth older sisters took over the parenting role. According to Kai-Ming, the third sister's status was now "almost equal" to the mother's. The fourth sister lost her position after she attempted suicide. She was seen as weak and immature, thus no longer a role model for the younger siblings.

The family was quite undifferentiated. Except for the father and younger brother, they were closely tied to one another, mutually interdependent, and merged. They were into one another's business. They felt responsible for one another's feelings and well-being. Their interdependence was intensified as an adaptation to immigration. Kai-Ming was favored by the parents, especially the mother, because he was the first boy born after she had four girls. The mother invested most of her emotions in him. He was catered to by his mother and his sisters, which reinforced his delay in autonomy.

Kai-Ming lost the father as an idealization figure, and he over-identified with the mother, with whom he had a symbiotic relationship. He felt responsible for her feelings and well-being. Adequate separation-individuation had not been achieved. He regressed when he felt threatened by separation from the mother. His mother indulged him and reinforced his dependency by not allowing him to make choices such as what clothes to wear, what places to go, and so forth. The intensity of his mother's feelings toward him made him more vulnerable, and he became susceptible to feelings of guilt.

The family resented Kai-Ming's presenting symptoms. They believed that he was just being silly and disobedient and was purposefully trying to upset the family. They believed that he could control his illness but was making no effort to do so. Therefore, they wanted to assert more disciplinary measures. They punished him by not talking to him and by scolding him, so he would "think it over" and regain his senses. Kai-Ming expressed that "they gang up against whoever does something wrong."

The patient's presumptive DSM III R diagnosis on admission was:

Axis I: Delusional (paranoid) disorder. He fitted the following diagnostic criteria for this disorder:

 A. Nonbizarre delusion(s), that is, involving situations that occur in real life such as growing nose, upward eyebrows, and contagious skin disease.

 B. No auditory or visual hallucinations.

 C. Apart from the delusions, he did not exhibit bizzare behavior.

 D. No major depression despite suicide ideation.

 E. Never has criteria A for schizophrenia

Axis II: Dependent personality disorder

TREATMENT PLAN

The initial goal was to engage Kai-Ming in psychotherapy. Although he did not have an active suicidal plan, he was at high risk for suicide. He had a history of prior resistance to treatment. Both Kai-Ming and his family had very poor insight into his illness. Therefore, the following objectives and approaches were planned:

 1. Request Kai-Ming to sign a contract for three months with a pledge not to act on suicidal impulses. Additionally, he would agree to come for treatment three times a week for the first month and twice a week for the subsequent two months. He would also need to be compliant to medication instructions.

2. Prescribe medication to eliminate his psychotic symptoms, especially his somatic delusions, which aggravate his suicidal rumination.

3. Provide brief psychosocial education to Kai-Ming and his family on the nature of his illness, treatments, and medication. Better understanding of these issues could reduce anxiety and motivate him and his family to follow through with the treatment.

4. The family is assigned the responsibility of ensuring Kai-Ming's compliance with treatment and medication until he can accept greater responsibility.

5. Provide supportive counseling to the family regarding management of Kai-Ming's daily routine and impulsive behavior.

6. Assist the family to apply for medicaid in view of their eligibility for this assistance.

The long-term goals are the following:

1. To eliminate psychotic symptoms.

2. Individual psychotherapy to facilitate separation/individuation process; resolve sexual-identity crisis; and resolve racial-identity crisis.

3. Short-term family therapy to initiate the separation/individuation process for all family members and to reconstruct the family structure to the normality accepted by the culture. The father should be assisted to regain his position of authority and share responsibility with the mother, thus reducing the burden of responsibility on the two older sisters. This would also help to provide Kai-Ming with a suitable male role model and to counteract the mother's pathological clinging to the patient.

TREATMENT SUMMARY

Kai-Ming was seen for pharmacotherapy and psychotherapy at our clinic for about one year. The family was seen in joint sessions on a consultation basis. During the treatment period, Kai-Ming was hospitalized twice for suicidal ideation. He began phasing out of treatment at the tenth month and requested termination two months later.

On the day of intake, Kai-Ming was asked to sign a contract pledging not to act on his suicidal impulses and to stay in treatment for at least three months. Subsequently he extended this contract three times. Here, compliance with authority, a cultural feature, was used to the advantage of therapy. In general, it is very difficult to contract with a paranoid patient because of the patient's suspiciousness. Contracting with this particular patient was possible because of the therapist's sensitivity to the cultural dynamics. This sensitivity enabled her to understand the patient's willingness to comply with authority in a therapeutic relationship.

Emphasizing the expertise of the treatment team, the therapist also enlisted the support of the entire family. Thus Kai-Ming reported that he had faith in treatment and wished to be cured.

Although the therapist had clarified that there was no guarantee that he would be cured and that the treatment team was making its best efforts to help him, after signing the contract, Kai-Ming claimed to have faith in treatment and hoped to be cured.

His extreme, concrete compliance with authority is evidenced in the following examples: At the second psychiatric evaluation after signing the contract, he responded to inquiry about his suicidal ideation by stating, "I won't kill myself because I have a contract with Ms. Ma." Yet at another time, out of frustration, he announced that he "could do anything (including suicide) when the contract is due." Thus, the contract provided limits for Kai-Ming, and he seemed comfortable under the protection of the authority.

The family also respected very much the therapist's authority. They readily accepted the assignment to monitor Kai-Ming's treatment and also requested consultation in other areas of their lives. At times, they would quote the Chinese psychiatrist and the therapist.

At the initial stage of the individual psychotherapy, Kai-Ming was obsessed with his somatic delusion and could only deal with it in a very concrete way. With the aid of brief psychosocial education on developmental issues and psychodynamics, the therapist was able to explore his identity crisis in growing up and in adapting to the new culture.

Although Kai-Ming was not able to relate his symptoms to the traumatic experience, he was in touch to some degree with his conflicts in both separation/individuation and racial identity. For example, he reacted to his mother's plan to visit his sisters in Hong Kong with regression in functioning. With some insight, he admitted it was possible that he became sick to keep his mother home and that he felt guilty about being "selfish" in that respect. Also, he stated that he wanted to look like an American yet he also wanted his "own beauty." He compared in detail the features of orientals and white Americans.

In order to facilitate the differentiation of Kai-Ming from his family, or rather, all the family members from one another, the family was consulted and invited to joint sessions. Efforts were made to reconstruct the family structure in order to remove the children from adult responsibilities and redefine each person's boundary.

The family-therapy model was unconventional. To be realistic and effective, the meeting frequency was irregular and determined by such needs of the family as crises, the work/school schedule, and the motives of each individual. Whoever could come was received whenever they could come, although they were still encouraged to be consistent and regular. This was felt to be of particular relevance to Asian Americans, who put their values and priority on work and education. Asking them to disrupt their work or school schedule would be counterproductive to the development of the therapeutic alliance.

In general, Kai-Ming gradually stabilized. He resumed his routine activities and full-time work in the factory.

Kai-Ming, however, reacted again with suicidal ideation when he was being forced by his family to return to school. When the second contract expired, he refused to renew it and was hospitalized shortly thereafter.

Although the hospital had been informed of Kai-Ming's suicidal ideation, the staff decided to discharge him after two weeks because he denied his suicidal ideation. Apparently, Kai-Ming's transference feelings toward the therapist (who is Chinese) as an authority encouraged him to honestly disclose his suicidal ideation to her. However, his feelings of alienation and lack of rapport with the "American" hospital staff probably prompted him to deny the ideation to them.

Kai-Ming was prescribed an antidepressant drug, a monoamine oxidose inhibitor (MAOI) upon discharge and was given a diet that listed fermented food products he needed to avoid because such food would interact negatively with the drug. However, the foods listed included only those that would appear in an American diet, not a Chinese one. He might have been in fatal danger if the Chinese psychiatrist had not provided him with a suitable Chinese diet. Even with the modified diet, he was finally advised to stop taking the MAOI because of his suicidal risk. It was also clear that the patient's home environment could not support him to abstain from undesirable foods.

The patient lost faith in treatment after a second hospitalization. The Chinese psychiatrist recommended electroconvulsive therapy during his two hospitalizations, as Kai-Ming did not respond well to various neuroleptics and antidepressants. However, both hospitals opposed the recommendation and informed the patient of all possible negative effects of the treatment. The patient became angry at the Chinese psychiatrist for suggesting such a "horrible" treatment to him and felt that he did not care about him.

Briefly, after the second discharge, Kai-Ming asked to stop medication. He became religious and visited a Chinese temple often. He decided to go back to school with the agreement of a follow-up visit with us after three months.

Kai-Ming dropped out of treatment after the last contract was due. He had been enrolled in school for about four months when he returned for two more appointments upon request. He complained about his computer class and asked to be removed from it. He requested termination. Six months later, the family reported that Kai-Ming was still attending school, though not consistently. He became increasingly religious and withdrawn again, but he refused to continue treatment.

CONCLUDING STATEMENT

The functioning of this family was disrupted by the immigration experience. The father became disengaged because of the necessity to work out of town. This deprived the patient of a mature male role model.

As an accompaniment to the immigration experience, the patient's struggle with identity issues, both sexual and racial, became more acute. A less cohesive family and community network made him more vulnerable to psychotic decompensation.

The cultural awareness of the treatment team is seen as a necessary ingredient for treatment of high-risk first-generation immigrants. In working with this particular Chinese American psychotic patient, cultural transference was employed successfully to foster the therapeutic alliance at an early stage. Furthermore, the empathy and sensitivity of the Chinese psychiatrist to cultural norms prevented a possible hypertensive crisis resulting from MAOI treatment.

In the therapist's opinion, although the patient withdrew from treatment and turned to the temple instead, he may actually find solace in religion. The temple might provide male figures (monks) whose authority is supreme and absolute, and with whom he can identify. This could help him form a less fragmented, more cohesive self.

DISCUSSION QUESTIONS

1. How does one effectively tease apart the extent to which a patient's problems are the product of stressful experiences such as immigration and discrimination versus a set of family dynamics that appear problematic?

2. Would some of the family dynamics that appear problematic within the context of American culture (i.e., the intense interdependence among family members) have appeared normative and proven non-problematic had the family remained in Hong Kong?

3. To what extent are biological forces interacting with environmental stressors and family dynamics in this case to produce what is actually the first manifestation of a schizophrenic disorder?

4. How does the structure of the therapy, that is, short-term individual therapy three times per week for three months extended on a contractual basis, play a role in the transference relationship with this client?

5. How did the client perceive the therapeutic relationship? How did sociocultural factors and family dynamics contribute to his perceptions? What was the basis of the therapist's credibility?

Bridging Generations and Cultures

Jennie H. Y. Yee

This case of a 24-year-old American-born Chinese female who was seen in outpatient psychotherapy following hospitalization for an acute psychotic episode illustrates how difficult it is for a young adult standing between two cultures to forge a personal identity. The client, who is referred to as Anna, was struggling to come to terms with her sense of herself as an autonomous and independent young woman and at the same time to remain true to her sense of what it means to be a good Chinese daughter. Anna both identified with her mother and felt enormous resentment toward both parents for the demands they made on her to subjugate her goals to the needs and desires of the family. Her anger and resentment and resulting guilt became so intense that she was hospitalized when she heard voices telling her that her family was going to be butchered and that she was going to die. Anna, who had a diagnosis of paranoid psychosis in remission, was seen in outpatient psychotherapy for three years by a Chinese-American therapist. The therapy was conducted in English.

The work in therapy centered on Anna's efforts to address issues of autonomy and of cultural and personal identity. Anna's need to find a way to make a healthy emotional separation from her mother was complicated by her mother's overinvolvement and tendency to be intrusive and overprotective. Anna's Caucasian boyfriend, whom she saw on the sly because her parents disapproved of his race, symbolized her struggle with her identity as a Chinese-American; she was pulled in different directions by two cultures, both of which have attractions for her. Anna's difficulty in college in a major selected by her parents, her role as an interpreter for parents who speak only Cantonese, and her conflicting feelings about her obligations and commitments to the family business all represent attempts to negotiate cultural demands and ego-development issues simultaneously.

The case highlights both problematic and facilitative aspects of a racial/ethnic transference. The fact that the therapist was also Chinese American no doubt contributed to an early negative transference. Anna felt a lot of anger toward her mother and two older sisters and saw the therapist as part of the system oppressing her and as intrusive, demanding, and hypercritical. Thus she wanted to quit therapy. At the same time, the therapist, also because she is Chinese American, became an anchor in reality for the client. The therapist's race facilitated the establishment of a corrective female-female relationship that did not necessitate rejection of the client's Chinese heritage. The establishment over time of a non-hierarchical relationship contributed in positive ways to the client's efforts to work on separation-individuation within the therapy. Mutual female relationships have a central place in traditional Asian culture and may have facilitated a non-hierarchical relationship between client and therapist.

Examination of countertransference issues was central to therapeutic success in this case. For example, sharing the experience of being a minority group member and wanting to overprotect the client from the demands of family obligations highlights the potential pitfalls of over-identification with racial/ethnic similarities.

Major Theoretical Orientation of Therapist: Eclectic.

Language Used by Therapist and Client: English.

PRESENTING PROBLEMS

Anna was hospitalized at Christmas for several days and rehospitalized on New Year's day for one month after experiencing an acute psychotic episode. She heard voices saying her family would be butchered and that she should die. Her family reported that she attacked her mother by hitting her on the head with her hand. Anna reported severe conflicts with parents and teachers at the local college. She feels everybody puts unreasonable "pressures and demands" on her and criticizes her excessively; she feels they're "all in a plot to hurt me." "Failures" at school paralyze her and prevent her from completing her studies in accounting. Her relationship with her boyfriend, conducted on the sly, has caused tremendous stress and mistrust.

HISTORY AND DEMOGRAPHIC DATA

Anna is a 24-year-old American-born Chinese female, the second youngest of seven children, all of whom are female except one. There is an age gap of seven years between her and the next eldest child. Her parents were born in China and primarily speak Cantonese. Birth and childhood history are unremarkable, although both Anna and her mother reported that Anna was distant from all her siblings except the youngest. Currently, three unmarried sisters still reside at home with Anna and their parents. The mother informed Anna when she was eight years old that she had considered aborting her but had ultimately decided not to. Anna alternately feels unwanted and rejected or overprotected by her mother. The mother never made a happy adjustment to American life. The father is described as "secretive, not trusting, and withdrawn" or as emotionally distant—a perception of many Asian fathers. Performance was adequate in pre-college schooling, although Anna thinks her grades should have been better. Both Anna and her family feel that she holds very high standards and expectations of herself and others. When Anna was 16 years old, her parents withdrew her from high school and put her to work for them in an out-of-town grocery store as a cashier. Prior to that for several years, the family owned a laundry where members of the family worked in rotating shifts. Using children as free labor in family-owned businesses is a common phenomenon among Chinese immigrants. Promises were made to financially support her choice of a college away from home as leverage against the resentment and anger Anna felt for missing a year in high school.

When the grocery failed, Anna returned to complete high school; but the promise was broken because her parents were bankrupt. Instead, she enrolled at the local community college, majoring in accounting, something she hated but felt forced to do at her parents' suggestion. During the period away from high school, Anna became involved with a divorced Caucasian male 25 years her senior. A surreptitious dating affair ensued and was carried on for five years without her parents' knowledge. Because her parents would disapprove of the interracial relationship, Anna devised an elaborate pattern of secretiveness and deceit. Just prior to her psychotic break, Anna had a series of failures in college and her relationship with her boyfriend became very conflictual.

FUNCTIONING AND MENTAL STATUS AT INITIAL EVALUATION

Anna is a very thin, 24-year-old Chinese American female. She came dressed in casual but very neat and stylish clothing. At the beginning of the interview, she exhibited facial grimaces and frowns. She averted her eyes from the therapist and made only fleeting eye contact. She sat very stiffly and on the edge of her chair. Her affect was mostly flat but progressed to an angry stance as she talked of perceived betrayals by people. Her speech was articulate and fluent, becoming quite loud, rapid, and punctuated when expressing angry feelings. Paranoid thinking was evident, including feelings that others "manipulate and control" her, although she was not psychotic. She was correctly oriented to time, place, and person. Judgment appeared narrow but fair; insight ranged from fair to good. She had problems making decisions for herself. Defenses included externalization, projection, rationalization, and withdrawal. Good ego defenses were apparent in the form of humor and delay of gratification.

Anna is bright and verbal. Her psychosis had remitted after she began taking 10 mg. of Haldol four times a day for several days and then 75 mg. of chlorpromazine for one day. No other psychotropic medication was used until her next psychotic episode six months later. Her social, educational, and occupational functioning had been impaired for approximately a year.

Anna had three hospitalizations in less than six months. Each episode was preceded by a pattern of symptoms: withdrawal, irritability, suspiciousness, especially with family members, and intense anger. She felt frightened and had delusions of family and self-destruction as well as world deluge. She failed in college because she perceived conspiracy, and this precipitated each hospitalization.

Anna maintains a very suspicious and rigid paranoid stance with a tendency to project blame. She tends to be overly judgmental of others and extremely sensitive to criticism and rejection. She harbors resentment for a long time, and her mistrust of people's intentions prevents her from developing intimate friendships. Her mother's overintrusiveness and the family's demands on Anna heighten the conflict between Chinese cultural values and American expectations. The family defends against the outside world by huddling together in suspicious withdrawal. Attempts to taste the forbidden fruit of American life were acted out in her secret relationship with her Caucasian boyfriend. In the beginning, this was in response to loneliness and rebellion; later, this represented her bitter struggle to flee from the family snare. The final straw was failure in college, which represented the final failure to establish an independent, acceptable, and successful lifestyle. Her family's exhortations against venturing too far away from home (i.e., the Chinese community) and imagined dangers in the "white devils" had come true. Her return to the family as a well person threatened the homeostasis of the family system. The family could feel safe only with Anna as dysfunctional.

DIAGNOSTIC FORMULATION

The patient's DSM III diagnosis was given as:

Axis I: 295.35 Schizophrenia, paranoid
                                 type, in remission

TREATMENT PLAN

Short-term goals were to help Anna trust the therapist and to privide ego-supportive psychotherapy to reduce paranoid thinking and bolster ego defenses. Individual sessions centered on severe family conflict, with family sessions introduced when Anna could tolerate it. Her mother was seen by a separate therapist. Slow reintegration of ego strengths to be manifested in school and social spheres was planned.

Long-term goals were to resolve issues of separation/independence and dependency needs; strengthen interpersonal skills and learning competence; develop insight about conflicts with authority and parental figures; and enhance risk taking and decision making for self-growth.

Frequency: (1) Individual psychotherapy was provided—one session per week for the first year, biweekly for three months, and once per month thereafter. Length of therapy was three years; (2) phenothiazine medication was continued on a daily basis together with 8 mg. Trilafon.

SUMMARY OF SESSIONS AND TREATMENT

The treatment was divided into two phases. The first phase was a six-month period, and the second phase was two years following a month's rehospitalization for another psychotic episode.

In the first nine sessions, Anna expressed a lot of anger toward the therapist, her mother, and two older, unmarried sisters living at home.

After her first session with a female psychiatrist who was similar in age to her mother, Anna noted that the meeting felt "strange and uncomfortable." She remarked that she did not need to come back for therapy because it might interfere with her finding work; Anna could not explain this further. Next, Anna announced a surprising discovery she had made about how her mother had severely and negatively influenced her own behavior: "I make some of the same faces she does. . . .When I looked in the mirror the other day . . ."

The similarity is that Anna does not look directly at people when talking to them. She emphasized how angry she feels, especially when her mother continually turns her back on Anna when Anna attempts to talk with her. Anna goes on with the wish that her family would understand her better but readily admits she herself cannot understand their behavior. "When I tell them to do things that are better for them, they don't take my advice." When I query her about what she wishes to change in her family, Anna cannot be specific except for not having her sister live at home and for her mother not telling her what to do. Anna became very agitated and angry at me in this and the next session.

At the beginning of session 9, Anna raised the issue of not needing to come back to therapy. I asked why she felt therapy was "part of the system." How? "The school . . . the hospital . . . the government all try to force me to do things . . . they're all part of the same system." I queried further. "They might tell each other about me . . . and they all say they're right." How? "They try to manipulate me into doing what I don't think is right." And how do you know you are right? "I know I'm right." What happens if you're not right? "Then I might as well be in the hospital." Then Anna adds: "At least I'm not always wrong." I point out that right and wrong was so polarized. What about looking at it as different perspectives? Anna felt strongly that everything was either right or wrong. I asked whether Anna felt controlled in therapy. She said no, but that she had a feeling that the therapist was part of the system. When I suggested we discuss these feelings of being controlled, Anna declined, asserting that she no longer had the intense "angry feelings anymore," so she did not need therapy. I explained that therapy was also for expressing good and other kinds of feelings, and I offered an appointment. Anna: "I may still not come." I left open the alternative of coming back in the future if she wanted. Unfortunately, I made a mistake and telephoned to change the appointment. Anna was very firm this time: "No, I'm not coming back." I wished her luck and again invited her to call if she needed to talk. The following week Anna called and asked for an appointment because she felt very angry at her sister that week. She attended two more sessions to vent anger about family double messages. Again, she terminated but said she would come if evening hours were available. One month later, I telephoned Anna about my evening hours, but she was not interested. Two months later Anna's mother called twice in two weeks to inform me of Anna's irritability, anger, and yelling at the family and packing a bag as if to leave. I called Anna the following week; she told me she was "fine" and was planning to return to college. No, she was not interested in therapy. Soon thereafter, Anna relapsed and was hospitalized for one month.

Dynamics

It is important to point out that just before my second session with Anna, her mother came to see me to express her own anguish and complicity in her daughter's illness and requested therapy with me. Of course it was contraindicated because of Anna's paranoia. An alternative therapist was offered to her, but she did not want to see someone else. The family history, so representative of many Chinese families in the United States, provided the greatest amount of information helpful to the analysis of Anna's psychotic breakdown. The key issue is independence/dependence—how to make a healthy emotional separation from the mother, the embodiment of Chinese culture. This generalizes to separating from family, culture, and authority figures who represent the parents symbolically. All other issues are subsidiaries of this primary developmental goal, which is also an issue of culture conflict. Anna needs to find her own viable identity as a Chinese American without suffering the potential negative consequences of being rejected by her Chinese family or failing in American society. Anna's mother's intrusiveness and overprotectiveness at the beginning of therapy and the subsequent meeting with the psychiatrist evoked a severe negative transference reaction and exacerbated Anna's paranoia. Anna's perceptions were distorted, and the therapist was also suspected to be part of the family system that identified her as the patient. The rigid parameters of the family system did not allow for easy entry into white society. All the children were recruited to protect and maintain the family ego mass for economic and social survival. The suspiciousness and fear experienced by her parents, especially after failing in a business bought from Caucasians, drove the family into desperate withdrawal. They sought to prevent Anna from venturing away to college. The family's cultural paranoia and confirmation of dangers outside cemented the defense mechanism. She made two attempts to break out: one was overt—to go away to college—but was subverted, and the other was covert—to date a white man. When only the secretive act of rebellion remained, it grew as a disease of subterfuge, erupting in the only way possible—as a full-blown paranoid episode. The family in reality did everything they could do to stop the relationship. Anna, in her paranoia, became so confused she could not continue with her boyfriend without risking being disowned by her family; yet, to relinquish her boyfriend was to risk losing the only hope she had left to separate from the negative elements of Chinese culture and to integrate into American society. Everything split into black and white. All authority figures were perceived as intrusive, demanding, and hypercritical. The boyfriend became an object of suspicion as well, confirming her parents' warnings. Anna dealt with her confusion and helplessness, a result of the family's effective sabotage and blocking, by polarizing the issues into wrong and right and then venting anger at objects who were "wrong." Because of her fragile defenses, Anna had to erect rigid perceptions to protect herself from losing all. For Anna, acceptance by and approval from her family were critical. The thematic issue of feeling controlled and judged by the family transferred into the therapeutic relationship immediately, and Anna took control by rejecting me, the therapist. Yet Anna was afraid of my disapproval and potential unspoken condemnation and asked to come back to therapy after having had an argument with her sister and mother. I, as the therapist, was not to be trusted for two reasons: for forming a perceived alliance with the mother by allowing the mother to see me; and for suggesting that Anna was ill and needed therapy. In addition, I was the symbolic sister she needed to extrude. Anna tested the therapist's support to ensure that she was the one in control and again asserted termination. I accepted it, but subsequent overtures aroused suspicion that I was making intrusive, judgmental evaluations of her. The therapist's confrontation with Anna and her rigid defenses were mistakes. She needed to know she was not being controlled. The ultimate crash into psychosis again was a result of her not having erected new ego defenses strong enough to fight and survive in a powerful and rigid system. Also, her expectation for the family to change was unrealistic.

In the next major segment of therapy post-hospitalization (44 sessions to date), Anna requested a male Caucasian therapist at the outset. I promised to check into the possibility but also asked her for an alternative, for example, a white female. Anna decided she would rather keep me as an alternative. Anna's first choice was not available, and she accepted me. Again a similar pattern emerged, with the mother coming to the therapist and crying hysterically. This time, I firmly referred her to another therapist, whom she currently continues to see. At the third session, Anna's mother accompanied her to the clinic. Anna, who appeared extremely depressed and fearful for the first time, was seen alone. She had been "feeling very paranoid and scared and I don't know why. . . . I thought you had told my sisters everything I've told you, but I know it was not true. . . . I feel everyone on the street knew about me. I'm very frustrated and don't know what to do with my life. . . . I don't trust anyone. . . . I slept with my mother last night because I was so scared." I reassured Anna that it will get better and that her awareness that her suspicions were unfounded was a sign of getting better. I also explained that her mother needed therapy and would be seeing someone else. In the fourth and fifth sessions, Anna was more stable and less paranoid. She made a sudden decision to marry her boyfriend and then began to feel "unsure." She did not know whether getting married meant "trying to get away from the family or not" and also wondered whether she should feel uncertain. She wondered whether her mother wanted her to be sick and dependent. We discussed her mother's treatment of Anna. Between the sixth and tenth sessions, Anna continued to express uncertainty, anger, and mistrust of her sisters for being unable to escape from home, her conflicts over traditional Chinese versus American values, her relationship with her boyfriend, and her ambivalence about medication (which she had continued to take for the past three years). During this period she got an offer from her boyfriend to move in with him. We discussed the pros and cons, and again I reassured her that confusion was a healthy response to intense conflicts and that her struggle to become independent from her mother was a process wrought with complex feelings. Anna cried for the first time about her mother. She admitted, "[my family] drives me crazy," and wondered, "How can I ever accept it?" In a subsequent session, she reported leaving home to live with her boyfriend without informing her family, except for her youngest sister. She did not give her new address to her family or therapist.

The dynamic issues in these 10 sessions centered on establishing an undeveloped trust for the therapist, acknowledging the sadness she felt about her family, and testing the ground for making her own decisions. Sensing support, she was able to assert some risk-taking, thereby freeing herself literally. Subsequent sessions began to take on another tone and shape. The focus was: (1) learning to survive without her family but with her boyfriend, who then became the nurturing caretaker; (2) dealing with the guilt feelings in leaving mother; and (3) acknowledging her own responsibility in life, that is, admitting that much of the pressure to comply with tradition was emanating from within herself. In the seventeenth session, after Anna had accomplished "breaking away" with my benign support and actual encouragement, she confronted me for the first time. Because an alliance had been formed in the therapeutic relationship, Anna admitted she felt I criticized her when I seemed to side with her teachers (first segment of therapy). I validated her perception, since I had not empathized with her anger; she then felt tremendous relief.

From that session on, therapy sailed into working on current and future goals rather than just past distortions. There were virtually no role models in her family who had successfully made it out into the world as independent people; she was the first. Anna became more relaxed, less tough on herself, and began to slowly heal from the losses. She initiated safe projects like aerobics and sewing and helped her boyfriend with clerical work for pay. By the twenty-ninth session she had made her first contact with her mother by mailing her a birthday card after a five-month hiatus. Although ambivalent feelings were aroused, Anna admitted, "I guess I care about her." Anna's mother asked me to thank her daughter at the following session. Anna was very happy to hear her mother's response and asked to switch to biweekly sessions, an indirect statement that she had improved. The final acceptance of the therapist (symbolically mother and Chinese culture, or the bridge between Anna and mother) occurred (1) when Anna told me she wanted to stay in therapy for a longer time, "because it seems nobody gives me encouragement. . . . Here I can say what I want and air my doubts"; and (2) when her mother left a letter for her in my box and Anna asked me to read it to her, since it was in Chinese. Although I could not read all the words, Anna primarily wanted to know if "she is telling me to be careful about my boyfriend. . . . I don't like that." I reassured her that her mother only expressed general feelings of concern and caring. Anna said, "I'm glad . . . I don't know why I was so worried" and then laughed. Her mother had accepted her rapprochement.

During the next two years Anna enrolled in a vocational training program for three months, was hired for a job immediately upon completion of the program, and has been working very success-fully since then. Her relationship with her boyfriend continues, and friendships have developed at work. No psychotic episodes have recurred for two years, medication continues, and several success-ful meetings with Anna's mother were conducted without negative cathexis. Anna was surprised to see that her mother had changed.

DISCUSSION QUESTIONS

1. How important is it for Asian American clients struggling with personal and cultural identity issues to see Asian American therapists? What would have transpired in therapy had this client seen either a

Chinese-born Asian therapist or a Caucasian therapist? How important was the gender of the therapist in this case?

2. Would family therapy have been helpful for this client either in combination with individual therapy or instead of it?

3. Discuss the concept of cultural paranoia and how to deal with it in the therapeutic relationship.

4. Would issues of autonomy and separation have been as difficult in the therapeutic relationship if the therapist had been an older female, a male? How might these issues have been expressed differently?

Part III

Conclusion

Linking Theory and Practice

Joan Huser Liem

This book has focused on transference and empathy in psychotherapy with Asian Americans. Both processes describe important ways
of relating that arise not only within the therapeutic relationship but
in all interpersonal relationships. Transference is more often associated with the ways clients relate to therapists, whereas empathy is
more often used to describe therapists' responses toward their clients, but, in fact, transference and empathy describe processes that
are available to both therapists and clients. Empathy has been
described as the process of understanding another person as he or
she really is. It is a way of perceiving everyday reality from the
vantage point of the other person, of experiencing it from within the
other person's experience. Transference, on the other hand, has been
represented as a distorted understanding of the other, an inability to
see the other as he or she truly is or to experience a situation as the
other experiences it because one's perception is distorted by projective identifications with the past. We all engage in projective identification to various degrees, and we all strive for a more empathic
appreciation of the others in our lives.

Asian clients have been observed to transfer into the therapeutic
relationship ways of relating that are the product of growing up in

a culture that is hierarchical in nature and has prescribed rules of conduct with authority figures. Often, therapists are related to as authority figures regardless of their attitudes and behavioral styles. This can have positive and negative consequences for the therapy. On the positive side, it means that clients are apt to defer to the authority of the therapist and comply with a prescribed medical regimen. Kai-Ming's therapist was able to capitalize on his unquestioning obedience to her authority to establish an agreement whereby he would not attempt to take his own life.

On the negative side, the tendency to view the therapist as an authority figure and to defer to his or her authority means that many clients develop a rather formal relationship with the therapist, whom they expect to be directive and prescriptive. They wait for communications to flow from the therapist to them rather than engaging in mutual exchange. Robert exhibited this tendency at times, indicating that he looked to the therapist to tell him what she thought and what he should do. He came to therapy with a fixed agenda and took copious notes on what his therapist had to say. In Robert's case, this way of relating was probably influenced by both cultural and intrapsychic needs. He was both a nomadic wanderer looking for a wise and charismatic leader to anchor him and a little boy who wanted a loving mother who would show him the route to self-acceptance. Tyler, Sussewell, and Williams McCoy (1985) affirm in their elaboration of the "ethnic validity model" of psychotherapy that our views of others and of the world are colored by culture, ethnicity, race, and sex as well as intrapsychic phenomena. Like Robert's, most of our subjective perceptions are, in part, a reflection of our unique individuality and, in part, a function of the social milieu and historical context in which we are socialized.

When therapists and clients share the same racial and ethnic background, empathic understanding may be enhanced, but therapists may also engage in projective identification with their clients, a process we typically refer to as countertransference. Anna's therapist clearly identified with her as an American-born daughter of immigrant parents. Her identification with Anna enhanced her ability to be empathic, but it also may have made it difficult to remain neutral and adopt an objective analytic posture as Anna acted out her rejection of her family and her role as a Chinese daughter. Similarly, Mr. Chan's therapist's empathic acceptance of his client's desire not to discuss personal or family matters may have caused him to hold back and not push his client hard enough to examine key issues that were at the root of his distress. On the other hand, both therapists may have been responding empathically to the real needs and limitations of their clients, responses that preserved and forwarded their working relationships with them.

How do therapists develop an empathic understanding of clients of a different culture? Jenkins (1985) notes that cultural differences between therapist and client are often stumbling blocks to establishing deep, meaningful relationships. Basch (1980) points out that the main basis that therapists have for understanding any client is their own personality and personal as well as professional experience. When therapist and client share the same cultural background, an initial bond is formed more easily. When they do not share the same cultural background, they must be alert to personal biases that get in the way of relationship building and be prepared to deal with them. In that case, Jenkins (1985) argues that "a therapist's straightforward and respectful inquiry about things not known communicates that soothing attitude of acceptance of the client's self and self-enhancing efforts that are prerequisite for relationship building and progress [in therapy]." (p. 340)

In the cases that have been presented in this book, the therapists and clients share for the most part similar cultural backgrounds. Nevertheless, the therapists all work to establish trusting relationships by coming to know their clients; by developing a full understanding of their language, their communication styles, their values, their social and cultural context, and their affective experiences. They encourage their clients to interpret the world for them and they try to enter into their clients' worlds. They also try to communicate their empathic understanding of their clients' worlds to them through the adoption of language and interaction styles that are familiar and comfortable for their clients. That is not to say that they do not sometimes fall short of fully understanding the meaning for their clients of statements made in the therapy. There is the occasional tendency on the part of some therapists to assume too quickly that they understand their client's experience and emotional state. Several examples of this exist in the cases (assuming that the exchange that took place has been presented in its entirety). For example, at one point in the therapy Robert tells Dr. Saito that he is furious at his father for sexually abusing his sisters. He says he is ashamed and that he blames himself. We never learn why he blames himself, however, because rather than probing further to understand why he feels guilty for something his father did, Dr. Saito reassures Robert that it was not his fault, but rather the result of "how messed up your father and your mother are." Reassuring someone and telling them not to feel guilty when they do is very different from trying to understand fully the feeling they are experiencing. Additional respectful questioning may have enabled the therapist to see the world more clearly through Robert's eyes and may have enhanced Robert's self-understanding in the process.

We are most grateful to the therapists who shared these cases with us and allowed us to use them to develop a richer and more sensitive understanding of Asian American clients in psychotherapy. Even though the four therapists came from cultural and ethnic backgrounds similar to those of their clients, they still had to deal with differences in their clients that present difficult challenges to their empathic abilities: Robert's biracial heritage, his childhood abuse, and his interests in pornography and preoccupations with sex surely presented challenges for a young, female Asian therapist. Understanding what it feels like to be an aging Chinese man who has hardly ventured outside of Chinatown cannot be easy for a young, American university-educated male therapist. Kai-Ming's fragile sexual identity and bizarre delusions are not easy to comprehend, nor are the complex family dynamics in Anna's background.

In the process of elaborating on the key concepts of transference and empathy, contributors to this book have also identified a

number of general issues that therapists must be aware of in doing psychotherapy with Asian American clients. In conclusion, we would like to highlight several of these general issues, linking them to the concepts of transference and empathy and illustrating them where possible by referring to the case material.

THE LACK OF FAMILIARITY WITH PSYCHOLOGICAL EXPLANATIONS OF DISTRESS

Asian Americans are less likely to utilize mental health services than are white Americans or other ethnic minority groups (President's Commission on Mental Health, 1978; Sue and Mc-Kinney, 1975). In addition, when they do seek treatment, they have been shown to be experiencing greater levels of distress than their white counterparts and to drop out of treatment far more quickly (Sue and McKinney, 1975; Shon & Ja, 1982). Several explanations have been offered for Asian Americans' underutilization of mental health services, including their lack of familiarity with psychological explanations of distress and with the process of psychotherapy.

Many Asian Americans tend to experience distress psychosomatically and to search for organic explanations for their difficulties. Mr. Chan is an excellent example of this tendency. He looked to medical professionals not mental health professionals to help him deal with his frequent chest pains and persistent fears about having a heart attack. He was determined to prove that his complaints had a legitimate biological basis and was initially unfamiliar with and skeptical of psychological explanations for his symptoms. It was important for his therapist to accept his biological orientation and to educate him about the relationship between psychological and biological phenomena in stress reactions. In a similar vain, Kai-Ming, the 17-year-old with somatic delusions, initially defined his psychological problem as a skin disease and sought the help of a dermatologist.

The "lack of psychological mindedness" manifested by many Asian American clients can sometimes be misinterpreted by ther-

apists as a form of resistance when in fact it reflects genuine cultural differences in how emotional distress is experienced and understood. Not only is there a tendency in Asian cultures not to separate mental from physical health but Stanley Sue (1976) has found that Asian Americans generally believe that mental health is maintained by avoiding bad thoughts and exercising willpower. Individuals experiencing psychological distress, then, are often thought by themselves and others as weak-willed. This view was clearly articulated by Kai-Ming's family, who believed that his symptomatic behavior was the product of disobedience and purposeful attempts on his part to upset them, not the manifestation of a serious psychological illness. They believed he could control his disturbed behavior and disciplined him by refusing to talk to him or by scolding him in an effort to encourage him to do so.

The tendency to view problems in biological terms or as fully under the individual's conscious control is most apparent in the two cases involving clients who were born in China, but even American-born Asian clients often lack familiarity with psychological processes. Even Robert, who was American born, and who sought out psychotherapy of his own volition, puzzled over how it worked and why.

Root (1985) makes a compelling argument that sensitivity to the cultural and ethnic heritage of Asian American clients, including their way of conceptualizing problems, is essential to engaging them in psychotherapy. Sue and Zane (1987) note that therapists who conceptualize problems in ways that are incongruent with clients' belief systems lose credibility in the eyes of their clients and often lose their clients to premature termination. One need not take this caution to mean that a therapist must never move beyond the client's way of conceptualizing his or her problems. It does mean, however, that therapists need to make every effort to achieve an empathic understanding of the client's construction of the problem situation, on both a cognitive and an emotional level, and to communicate that understanding using language and concepts that are familiar to the client. Offering the client alternative ways

of thinking about problems can then go on in an educational context that is respectful of the client's perspective.

THE LACK OF FAMILIARITY WITH PSYCHOTHERAPY

Many Asian clients who are seen in psychotherapy have had no previous contact with mental health service providers. They have had experience with the medical establishment and often enter therapy, as did Mr. Chan, expecting the therapist to function much like a medical doctor. It becomes necessary for therapists working with such clients to acknowledge the clients' expectations and to educate them about the ways in which psychotherapy differs from the practice of medicine and the therapist's role differs from the role of the medical doctor (Root, 1985).

D. W. Sue (1981) has outlined a number of ways in which traditional psychotherapy practices stand in direct contrast with Asian cultural patterns and are thus likely to be confusing to Asian American clients. First, there is a strong tendency in Western models of therapy to distinguish between physical and mental health. For many Asian Americans, as stated previously, physical and mental health are not viewed as separate phenomena. Second, self-disclosure and direct communication of feelings are emphasized in Western forms of therapy. In many Asian cultures feelings are expressed indirectly, and restraint is valued in discussions about oneself or one's family. In addition, most Western models of therapy emphasize independence and focus on helping the individual develop an increased sense of autonomy, while many Asian cultures place a high value on interdependence and maintenance of strong ties to one's family. Thus many of the values inherent in Western therapy models may be unfamiliar, confusing, or even distasteful to Asian American clients. Therapists need to make sure that they are clear about the expectations that clients bring into psychotherapy and the ways in which those expectations may differ from their own. Taking the time to inform themselves fully about their Asian American clients' expectations and to educate their clients about the nature of psychotherapy and how it works can be critical to the formation of a therapeutic alliance and to successful treatment.

Interpreting transference is often a central feature of psychotherapy as it is practiced by Western therapists. The concept of transference and the process of examining the clients' perceptions of and feelings and attitudes toward the therapist are likely to be quite unfamiliar to Asian American clients. The importance of examining the clients' relationship to the therapist may not be immediately apparent to the client. Its value to the therapeutic process may need to be explained and elaborated over time just as Mr. Chan's therapist explained and elaborated the body-psyche-stress relationship to his client.,

Therapists working with clients from different cultural backgrounds must challenge themselves to make explicit the assumptions on which their practice of therapy is based and to ascertain whether these are assumptions their clients share.

SHAME AND STIGMA ASSOCIATED WITH MENTAL ILLNESS IN ASIAN CULTURES

Because there is a tendency to associate mental health with thinking positive thoughts and exercising willpower and mental illness with personal weakness, a great deal of shame is associated with manifestations of mental distress. Asian Americans who experience emotional problems tend to feel that they have failed not only themselves but their families, a view often reinforced by their families and their community.

Asian families are expected to be able to solve their personal problems; therefore, seeking help for problems outside the family is an act that has the potential to bring disgrace to the family. Families often do not seek services for mentally ill members because they feel that to do so would reflect poorly on their parenting skills and stigmatize them within the larger community. Therapists need to be especially sensitive to the shame and stigma associated with mental illness and lesser manifestations of emotional distress in many Asian communities. This sense of shame was apparent in Mr. Chan's need to prove that he was not crazy and that his symptoms had a legitimate biological basis. It was also apparent in Mr. Chan's desire not to show his weaknesses in front of his wife during the one joint session that was held by the therapist.

Robert expressed his shame when he indicated to the therapist that there were things about himself that he was afraid to reveal because if she knew them she would think there was something terribly wrong with him, that he was "damaged" and she would reject him. Robert articulated very clearly one not uncommon Asian perspective on things psychological when he said that his mother thinks that "psychology is the Devil's work."

Anna's ambivalence about seeking help through psychotherapy was manifested through her several efforts to terminate the process and her expression of concern that the therapist had told her sisters about what they had discussed in therapy and that "everyone in the street knew about [her]."

Preoccupation with the stigmatizing nature of mental illness is not unique to Asian clients. Even the most sophisticated psychotherapy clients are uncomfortable about admitting to their treatment in some circles and with good reason, as the public treatment of psychiatric histories among political candidates demonstrates. Therapists need to be especially sensitive, however, to the extent to which the stigma becomes a source of family shame for Asian clients. Many Asian clients and their families come to therapy, when they come at all, with a strong need for confidentiality that is intimately tied to the shame they feel at being unable to resolve their own difficulties. Kim (1985) notes that it can be useful for the therapist to acknowledge and reframe this need. Instead of interpreting a preoccupation with confidentiality as a sign of an inability to trust the therapist as might typically be the case, the therapist might point out to family members that it is evidence of the strength they possess as a family that they are able to seek help in spite of strong cultural prohibitions against doing so. Reluctance of individual clients to discuss family matters in therapy may reflect, at least in part, the individual's empathic understanding of the family shame that has resulted from his or her personal distress.

THE CENTRAL ROLE OF THE FAMILY IN ASIAN CULTURES: IMPLICATIONS FOR PSYCHOTHERAPY

In most Asian cultures family bonds are multigenerational and enormously strong. Ties to the past are preserved through memories of and tributes to ancestors. There is a tendency to be past rather than future oriented and to place great emphasis on preserving harmony between past and present relationships. Whereas individual identity is often derived in Western cultures from personal achievement, in Asian cultures, identity is derived from one's family membership. As a result, there is less of a tendency to strive for independence and self-direction and a much greater tendency to be motivated by a desire to comply with and forward the goals, aspirations, and norms of the family.

These differences in cultural values complicate the ways in which therapists need to think about the relationship between their clients and their families. Issues of separation and individuation, frequent focal points in psychotherapy with young adults like Robert, Anna, and Kai-Ming, become complicated in the context of the interdependence of Asian family members. Hess and Handel (1972), writing about dynamics that are characteristic of "all" family units, discuss the tension that exists in families as they struggle to balance the needs for separateness and connectedness among family members. How families work out the amount of separateness and connectedness among family members is heavily influenced by culture as well as by individual family dynamics. Kai-Ming's and Anna's therapists talk about the overinvolvement of Kai-Ming's mother and sisters and Anna's mother in the lives of their clients, but overinvolvement needs to be understood and evaluated in the context of Asian, not American, cultural norms. Therapists working with Asian American clients need to be aware of the natural support networks that exist within the extended family and the Asian community as a whole. Clients who turn to family members and other friends and relatives for help with their problems are not diluting the process of therapy or acting out. They are simply activating long-standing means of support that are familiar to them and have served them well in the past.

It would not be unusual for an Asian American client to expect his therapist to be involved with and available to his whole family or to include other family members in problem-solving efforts. It is because of the centrality of the Asian family within the culture that family therapy has often been suggested as the intervention of choice for Asian Americans.

Shapiro (1988) describes the normative challenges confronted by parents as children mature and change and present parents with new ways of being that require new responses from them. She notes that a climate of safety, a sense of personal competence, and the experience of some control over one's environment are necessary in order for family members to be responsive to changes in one another and in the nature of their relationships. Immigration is not an experience that contributes to a climate of safety that makes it possible for parents to be open to healthy changes in their offspring. The acculturation process is itself a process of change. It requires giving up much that is familiar and embarking on much that is new. It often generates a great deal of stress within families, making it difficult for them to respond to normative developmental changes in the children through flexible and complementary changes in the adult family members. Suggestions of such difficulties are present in the descriptions of both Kai-Ming's and Anna's families. Both families turn inward to protect themselves against the stresses and affronts to their dignity and competence caused by life in a strange land. Both sets of parents have difficulty using their knowledge of themselves as children in their families of origin to help them understand and support their children as they grow and change. They must learn to deal simultaneously with the normal maturational changes in their children and the socioenvironmental influences that are shaping those changes, a demand that in each case taxes the family system. It is important for therapists to be sensitive to the special challenges that immigrant families face as they negotiate the usual life cycle issues that confront all families.

SOCIOENVIRONMENTAL STRESSORS: THE CONTEXT FOR PSYCHOTHERAPY WITH ASIAN AMERICANS

Racism, discrimination, language barriers, immigration traumas, and financial problems often complicate the process of development for Asian Americans and other minority individuals. Mr. Chan, Kai-Ming's father, and Anna's parents, as first-generation immigrants, all confronted limited occupational opportunities, financial constraints, and the problems of learning a new language and culture. Kai-Ming was harassed because he was one of only a few Asian students in his school. His family and Anna's were still struggling with the financial burdens of immigration and limited employment opportunities. Robert experienced discrimination from both the Black and Asian communities and felt accepted by neither because of his biracial heritage. Socioenvironmental stressors make more difficult the challenges of negotiating normal developmental transitions for both individuals and their families. This is the social context in which therapy takes place and about which the therapist needs to be empathic. It is a context that, as Chin points out, inevitably influences the therapeutic alliance and transference relationship.

BICULTURALISM: A CRITICAL CHARACTERISTIC OF ASIAN AMERICAN CLIENTS

For each of the four clients discussed in the case material, the issue of cultural identity is critical. Robert's identity confusion arises in large part because he is the product of two very different cultures, African and Asian, neither of which welcomes him as a full participant. He must find ways of integrating and expressing his biracial heritage in the absence of an easily identifiable and supportive community to help him with his struggle.

Mr. Chan maintains a strong sense of pride in his Chinese heritage. He has chosen to preserve his Chinese identity as fully as possible and to keep the Western culture in which he resides at a considerable distance. This works fairly well for him because of his residence in Chinatown, but it begins to be more problematic as the influences of American culture start to have an impact on his life through the growing independence of his wife and daughters. The changes in them and their way of being in the family, changes no doubt brought about by their exposure to American society, contribute to Mr. Chan's anxiety.

Anna struggles directly with the conflicts inherent in a bicultural identity. American-born and educated, she finds that she needs to give voice to her growing desire for more autonomy. At the same time, she feels bound by the obligations that are associated with being a good Chinese daughter. Bridging two cultures becomes so difficult for her that she has to leave one entirely, at least temporarily, in order to succeed in the other.

Kai-Ming, the most troubled of the four clients, manifests his cultural-identity struggles through his somatic delusions. He fantasizes himself acquiring Caucasian physical characteristics.

Each of the four clients and their families wrestle in their own ways with their biculturalism. They must work out how many aspects of their original cultural heritage to maintain and how many aspects of their new cultural home to take on. Immigrant generations differ in their choices from the first generation born in the United States, and they in turn differ from subsequent generations. Exploring fully the choices clients make about the nature of their acculturation can be an important part of understanding who they are. It is a critical element in the therapy process with Asian American clients.

Working with clients from different cultural backgrounds can be enormously challenging, but it can also be enormously growth promoting for clients and therapists alike. Our goal in this book has been to locate two essential clinical processes, transference and empathy, within the Asian cultural context. In doing so, we have tried to facilitate the further development of both cultural and clinical competence for psychotherapists and those persons endeavoring to become psychotherapists.

EXERCISES

Learning the practice of psychotherapy comes not from reading alone, but also from those experiential and didactic exercises which promote thought and affect. It is with this intent that we offer the reader exercises which, hopefully, will evoke thought, reflection, and affect.

Experiential Exercises

This book has provided theoretical concepts and extensive clinical material on four clients. Rather than accept what we have presented, the reader is now invited to use the material as background to role-play and videotape a replay of the presumed therapeutic process.

1. Role-play the client-therapist relationship as presented in the case materials. Videotape this and discuss the role play from the standpoint of transference and empathy.

2. Vary the therapist either by ethnicity, age, or sex. Role-play the client-therapist relationship again. Compare and contrast the process. Discuss the different manifestations of transference and empathy. You may want to do the role play again varying a second characteristic of the therapist.

3. In addition, observe and discuss the following as you view the role play or videotaped role play. Note especially differences which may be a function of ethnicity, age, or sex of the client or therapist:

    a.   Differences in verbal and nonverbal communication.

    b.   Differences in the therapeutic process.

    c.   Feelings evoked as you observe the interaction.

    d.   Subjective feelings of the actors during the role play.

Didactic Exercises

Take the written case material, vary one characteristic of the therapist (e.g., ethnicity, age, sex). Write or discuss how the process and outcomes of the case might be different. In particular, what forms might the transference relationship take? How is the therapist's empathic understanding of the client affected?

GENERAL DISCUSSION QUESTIONS

1. Identify the ways in which transference is manifested across the cases. Are there ways in which these manifestations are uniquely tied to the culture?

2. What form did empathy take in the various case presentations? How did the therapists make use of culture in developing it?

3. The clients seen by Hong and Ma are first-generation Asian Americans, whereas the clients seen by Yee and Saito are second-generation Asian Americans. Discuss similarities and differences in client presentation and therapeutic technique. Relate your observations to the client's immigrant versus American-born status. What appeared to be most helpful in each of the cases and why? How was resolution of the cases similar and different? Did the therapists differ in how directive they were in making psychotherapeutic suggestions?

4. All four therapists reporting cases are Asian American. To what extent were they serving as role models for their clients? Would the outcome of the cases be the same if the therapists were non-Asian American psychotherapists?

5. The chapters in Part I refer to the value placed on interrelatedness in many Asian cultures and contrast it with the emphasis placed on independence and autonomy within Western cultures. In several of the case studies as well, tensions between Western desires for independence and Eastern desires to remain closely connected to family seem critical. Given the different values placed on independence versus interrelatedness in different cultures, how do therapists make judgments about what constitutes parental overinvolvement or excessive dependency in a client? In general, how do decisions get made about what is pathological for a client who is bicultural?

6. Based on your reading of the cases and the theory chapters, what psychotherapeutic techniques seem most effective with Asian American clients?

7. Contrast the early phase of the therapeutic relationship with the latter phase in each of the cases. What observations might be generated regarding help-seeking behaviors, symptom manifestation, therapist credibility, and therapeutic effectiveness?

8. Does similarity of race and culture between therapist and client increase the risk that either participant in therapy will overidentify with the other? Will the therapist and client too quickly assume that he or she understands what the other is thinking and feeling:? How are these and other relational issues illustrated in the various case presentations?

9. Are there particular theoretical frameworks that are most facilitative in psychotherapy with Asian Americans?

10. Understanding what it means to be bilingual and bicultural is perhaps one of the most important challenges facing therapists who work with ethnic minority clients. When there is a conflict, how can therapists facilitate coping with the conflicting demands of biculturalism?

11. How can future therapists be trained to understand the experience of biculturalism? Family-therapy training programs often have trainees explore their own family histories and dynamics. Would it be helpful for therapists to explore their ethnic heritage and its influence on their lives however many generations removed? Does learning a second language facilitate cultural empathy? How important is foreign travel and work within ethnic communities?

12. The term Asian American includes people from different national, ethnic, and cultural heritages. How do such differences affect the issues of transference and empathy? Are the commonalities among different groups, especially their common identity as the Asian American minority in this country, strong enough to override their differences?

REFERENCES

Basch, M. F. (1980). *Doing psychotherapy*. New York: Basic Books.

Hess, R. D., & Handel, G. (1972). The family as a psychosocial organization. In G. Handel (Ed.), *The psychosocial interior of the family*. Chicago: Aldine.

Jenkins, A. H. (1985). Attending to self-activity in the Afro-American client. *Psychotherapy* [Special issue: Psychotherapy with ethnic minorities], 22(2), 335–341.

Kim, S. C. (1985). Family therapy for Asian Americans: A strategic structural framework. *Psychotherapy* [Special issue: Psychotherapy with ethnic minorities], 22(2), 342–348.

President's Commission on Mental Health. (1978). Report of the President. Washington, DC: U.S. Government Printing Office.

Root, M. (1985). Guidelines for facilitating therapy with Asian American clients. *Psychotherapy* [Special issue: Psychotherapy with ethnic minorities], 22(2), 349–356.

Shapiro, E. R. (1988). Individual and family development: Individuation as a family process. In C. Falicov (Ed.), *Family transitions: Continuity and change over the life cycle*. New York: The Guilford Press.

Shon, S. P., & Ja, D. Y. (1982). Asian families. In M. McGoldrick, J. K. Pearce, & J. Giordano (Eds.), *Ethnicity and family therapy* (pp. 208–228). New York: The Guilford Press.

Sue, D. W. (1981). *Counseling the culturally different: Theory and practice*. New York: Wiley.

Sue, S. (1976). Conceptions of mental illness among Asian- and Caucasian-American students. *Psychological Reports*, *38*, 703–708.

Sue, S., & McKinney, H. (1975). Asian Americans in the community mental health care system. *American Journal of Orthopsychiatry*, 45(1), 111–118.

Sue, S., & Zane, N. (1987). The role of culture and cultural techniques in psychotherapy: A critique and reformulation. *American Psychologist*, *42*(1), 37–45.

Tyler, F. B., Sussewell, D. R., & Williams McCoy, J. (1985). Ethnic validity in psychotherapy. *Psychotherapy* [Special issue: Psychotherapy with ethnic minorities], 22(2), 311–320.

Annotated Bibliography

Asian-American Community Mental Health Training Center. (1983). *Bridging cultures: Southeast Asian refugees in America.* Los Angeles: Special Service for Groups.

This text is composed of five sections that explore theoretical and social policy issues, as well as economic issues and health service approaches for Southeast Asian populations.

Boehnlein, J. K. (1987). Culture and society in posttraumatic stress disorder: Implications for psychotherapy. *American Journal of Psychotherapy, 41*(4), 519–530.

This article presents comprehensive methods of cross-cultural psychotherapy for posttraumatic stress disorder (PTSD). These include cultural belief systems and traditional family and social role expectations. The methods are illustrated with the use of case studies.

Bokan, J. A., and Campbell, W. (1984). Indigenous psychotherapy in the treatment of a Laotian refugee. *Hospital and Community Psychiatry, 35*(3) 281–282.

This article focuses on a case report describing how Western psychotherapeutic techniques were used in conjunction with a traditional Laotian healing ritual in the treatment of a Laotian refugee with a psychotic depression.

Brower, I. C. (1983). Counseling Vietnamese. In Asian-American Community Mental Health Training Center (Eds.), *Bridging cultures: Southeast Asian refugees in America* (pp. 224–240). Los Angeles: Special Service for Groups.

Vietnamese immigrants who have recently arrived in the United States are frequently affected by the repercussions of over thirty years of war and refugee experiences. These war-related traumas, combined with the already significant cultural differences, pose special problems for the Vietnamese. This article attempts to help counselors become sensitized to these unique problems.

Chin, J. L. (1990). Transference and countertransference issues as related to gender and ethnicity with Asian Americans. *The Clinical Psychologist, 43*(5), 67–69.

A case study that outlines the development of transference over a three-year period of psychotherapy with an Asian couple is used in this article to challenge some of the common myths about psychotherapy with Asian Americans.

Chu, J., & Sue, S. (1984). Asian/Pacific Americans and group practice. *Social Work with Groups, 7*(3), 23–36.

Many Asian/Pacific Americans do not utilize mental health services because traditional Western methods are insensitive to their mental health needs. The authors discuss various strategies for effective psychotherapy with these groups that consider cultural and historical implications.

Endo, R., Sue, S., & Wagner, N. N. (Eds.). (1980). *Asian Americans: Social and psychological perspectives*, Vol. III. Palo Alto, CA: Science and Behavior Books.

The companion to the 1973 text *Asian Americans: Psychological perspectives*, this volume presents a comprehensive exploration of "adaptations" or current developments made within the Asian American Community as Asian Americans become acculturated to life in contemporary American society. The text comprises four parts: (1) patterns of individual and family adaptation; (2) patterns of community and group adaption; (3) contemporary issues; and (4) perspectives of research.

Gaw, A. (1982). *Cross-cultural psychiatry*. Boston: John Wright–PSG.

Section one of this book comprises four chapters on cultural aspects of mental health care for Asian Americans aimed at increasing the clinician's understanding of the cultural implications of therapy with Asian Americans.

Ham, M. D. (1989). Empathic understanding: A skill for "joining" with immigrant families. *Journal of Strategic and Systemic Therapies, 8*(2), 36–40.

In the treatment of immigrant families, the family therapist needs to understand and know multiple world views: the perspective of the therapist, the perspective of the immigrant families, and the shared experience of both therapist and immigrant family. This article integrates base material with theoretical concepts to support this hypothesis.

Hong, G. K. (1988). A general family practitioner approach for Asian American mental health services. *Professional Psychology: Research & Practice, 19*(6) 600–605.

The author espouses an approach to therapy with Asian Americans in which the therapist functions as a primary-care provider in much the same way as does a family practitioner. Through ongoing interaction with the family, the therapist becomes a resource who can be consulted when difficulties arise. The application of this method is presented through the use of case studies.

Hong, G. K. (1989). Application of cultural and environmental issues in family therapy with immigrant Chinese Americans. *Journal of Strategic and Systematic Therapies* [Special issue], *8* (Summer), 14–21.

This article presents strategies developed by the author in providing treatment for Asian American families that address their unique cultural and acculturation issues. Examples of therapeutic interventions are provided with the use of case studies.

Hsu, J. (1985). The Chinese family: Relations, problems and therapy. In W. Tseng and D. Y. Wu (Eds.), *Chinese culture and mental health* (pp. 95–110). Orlando, FL: Academic Press.

Hsu explores Chinese family structure and the formative role the Chinese family plays in an individual's life. Psychological implications as well as recommendations for clinical procedures are presented.

Hsu, J., Tseng, W. S., Ashton, G., McDermott, J. F., Jr., & Chan, W. (1985). Family interaction patterns among Japanese American and Caucasian families in Hawaii. *American Journal of Psychiatry, 142*(5), 577–581.

This article details the results of a study in which the family interaction patterns of healthy Japanese American and Caucasian families were analyzed. The results indicate the need to "establish a culturally relevant family interaction profile" to prevent misrepresentation of the interactions of families who are outside the mainstream as being pathological.

Kim, S. C. (1983). Ericksonian hypnotic framework for Asian Americans. *American Journal of Clinical Hypnosis, 25*(4), 235–241.

The author espouses an Ericksonian framework for psychotherapy that includes "pacing," providing directives, and indirect suggestions as being more compatible with the cultural influences that often affect therapy with Asian Americans.

Kim, S. C. (1985). Family therapy for Asian Americans: A strategic structural framework. *Psychotherapy* [Special issue: Psychotherapy with ethnic minorities], *22*(2), 342–348.

The author proposes an integrated family therapy approach that combines strategic and structural interventions as a model that addresses the unique therapeutic needs of Asian Americans.

King, A. Y., & Bond, M. H. (1985). The Confucian paradigm of man: A sociological view. In W. S. Tseng & D. Y. Wu (Eds.), *Chinese culture and mental health* (pp. 29–42). Orlando, FL: Academic Press.

This article operates on the premise that Confucian values have played a significant role in shaping Chinese character. An analysis of the Confucian paradigm of man supports two conclusions: (1) Confucianism as a social theory tends to mold the Chinese into family-oriented beings, and (2) those family-oriented beings are also "capable of asserting a self-directed role in constructing a social world."

Kinzie, J. D. (1981). Evaluation and psychotherapy of Indochinese refugee patients. *American Journal of Psychotherapy, 35(2), 251–261*.

Based on his clinical experience with 70 Indochinese refugees, the author has drawn conclusions about the complexities of the initial evaluation of Indochinese refugees. Case studies are presented and strategies for successful therapy are discussed.

Kinzie, J. D., Leung, P., Bui, A., Ben, R., Keopraseuth, K. O., Riley, C., Fleck, J., & Ades, M. (1988). Group therapy with Southeast Asian refugees. *Community Mental Health Journal, 24*(2), 157–166.

> The authors describe the establishment of a one-year program of psychotherapy with groups of Southeast Asian refugees and the lessons learned as a result of the experience. They conclude that group therapy with Asian Americans can be successfully undertaken as a part of a comprehensive program of treatment.

Landau, J. (1982). Therapy with families in cultural transition. In M. McGoldrick, J. K. Pearce, & J. Giordano (Eds.), *Ethnicity and family therapy* (pp. 552–572). New York: The Guilford Press.

> The author outlines a model for therapy with families in cultural transition called "link therapy." This process involves coaching a member of the family who acts as a therapist within his or her own family.

Lappin, J., & Scott, S. (1982). Intervention in a Vietnamese refugee family. In M. McGoldrick, J. K. Pearce, & J. Giordano (Eds.), *Ethnicity and family therapy* (pp. 453–491). New York: The Guilford Press.

> The authors present the results of a successful, culturally sensitive therapeutic session with a Vietnamese refugee family in which dysfunctional mechanisms were altered without impeding the family's unique cultural elements.

Le, Q. T. (1983). Case illustrations of mental health problems encountered by Indochinese refugees. In Asian-American Community Mental Health Training Center (Eds.), *Bridging cultures: Southeast Asian refugees in America* (pp. 241–258). Los Angeles: Special Service for Groups.

> The numbers of Indochinese refugees who utilize mental health services is only a small fraction of the total Indochinese immigrant population. This article explains the discrepancies between the demands for and the use of mental health services. A profile of those immigrants who utilize the services of a mental health outpatient clinic geared specifically toward Asians is provided, as well as answers to the questions non-Indochinese mental health workers have on how best to treat refugees.

Lee, E. (1982). A social systems approach to assessment and treatment for Chinese American families. In M. McGoldrick, J. K.

Pearce, & J. Giordano (Eds.), *Ethnicity and family therapy* (pp. 527–551). New York: The Guilford Press.

The author provides practical guidelines for a social systems approach to therapy with Chinese American families that consider the person, his or her family, and other significant relationships. Two major social systems, the client system and the treatment system, are identified, and specific actions for therapeutic interventions are suggested.

Leong, F. T. (1986). Counseling & psychotherapy with Asian Americans: Review of the literature. *Journal of Counseling Psychology*, *33*(2), 196–206.

This article presents a comprehensive summary and critical analysis of the counseling and psychotherapy literature on Asian Americans. It is divided into three sections: (1) diagnostic and assessment issues; (2) counseling and psychotherapy; and (3) therapy process and outcome. In addition, suggestions are made for possible directions for future research.

Li-Repac, D. (1980). Cultural influences on clinical perception: A comparison between Caucasian and Chinese American therapists. *Journal of Cross-Cultural Psychology*, *11*(3), 327–342.

This article details the results of a study aimed at determining the extent to which cultural bias impedes a therapist's empathy and sensitivity.

Lorenzo, M. K., & Adler, D. A. (1984). Mental health services for Chinese in a community health center. *Social Casework*, *65*(10), 600–609.

This article describes the attempts of a mental health center to provide culturally effective treatment for Chinese Americans. Western modalities of psychotherapy adapted to consider Chinese cultural issues are used in an attempt to meet the needs of both nonpsychotic and psychotic Chinese patients.

McGoldrick, M., Pearce, J. K., & Giordano, J. (Eds.). (1982). *Ethnicity and family therapy*. New York: The Guilford Press.

This book identifies important cultural differences among ethnic and racial groups that have an impact upon the effectiveness of family therapy. The authors present cultural profiles of a variety of ethnic and racial groups and their relationship to specific intervention strategies.

Nishio, K., & Bilmes, M. (1987). Psychotherapy with Southeast Asian clients. *Professional Psychology: Research & Practice, 18(4), 342–346.*
    This article analyzes the problems of a growing Southeast Asian immigrant population that is unserved by American mental health services. Case studies and recommendations for psychotherapeutic interventions with Southeast Asian Americans are presented.
Root, M.P.P. (1985). Guidelines for facilitating therapy with Asian American clients. In G. R. Dudley & M. R. Rawlins (Eds.), *Psychotherapy* (Special issue: Psychotherapy with ethnic minorities), *22(2),* 349–356.
    This article recognizes a lack of sensitivity on the part of therapists to the cultural and ethnic heritage of Asian and Pacific Americans as a primary reason why these populations underutilize mental health services.
Shon, S. P., & Ja, D. Y. (1982). Asian families. In M. McGoldrick, J. K. Pearce, & J. Giordano (Eds.), *Ethnicity and family therapy* (pp. 208–228). New York: The Guilford Press.
    The authors present a profile of Asian families in an attempt to familiarize the therapist with the implications of cultural factors on the therapeutic process. Topics included are the Asian family structure, issues of obligation and shame, communication process, and the effects of cultural adaptation. In addition, suggestions for successful therapeutic interventions are presented.
Sue, S., & Morishima, J. K. (1982). *The mental health of Asian Americans.* San Francisco: Jossey-Bass.
    As a comprehensive analysis of Asian American mental health issues, this book is of value to practitioners, researchers, and graduate students who work with or are interested in the unique issues associated with providing therapy for Asian American populations.
Toupin, E. (1980). Counseling Asians: Psychotherapy in the context of racism and Asian American history. *American Journal of Orthopsychiatry, 50(1),* 76–86.
    This article considers the implications of the historical experiences of Asian Americans for counseling and psychotherapy. In working with Asian Americans, the author suggests careful consideration of the clients' migration experiences to America,

the effects of public education on second-generation immigrants, and cultural norms that impede acculturation.

True, R. H. (1990). Psychotherapeutic issues with Asian American women. *Sex Roles, 22*(7–8), 477–486.

This article discusses the unique issues relevant to providing counseling services for Asian American women. Therapeutic interventions are discussed with case studies and suggestions for therapists.

Tseng, W., & Wu, D. Y. (Eds.). (1985). *Chinese culture and mental health.* Orlando, FL: Academic Press.

An in-depth exploration of a variety of areas of Chinese culture and their implications for providing therapy for Chinese Americans. Topics include: Chinese concepts of personality, attitudes about mental illness, family issues, adaptation and coping mechanisms, and differences between Chinese and Western psychotherapy.

Tsui, A. M. Psychotherapeutic considerations in sexual counseling for Asian immigrants. In G. R. Dudley & M. R. Rawlins (Eds.), *Psychotherapy* (Special issue: Psychotherapy with ethnic minorities), *22*(2), 357–362.

The unique cultural implications of sexual counseling with Asian Americans are discussed, and recommendations for therapeutic interventions are presented.

Tsui, P., & Schultz, G. L. (1985). Failure of rapport: Why psychotherapeutic engagement fails in the treatment of Asian clients. *American Journal of Orthopsychiatry, 55*(4), 561–569.

In order to work effectively with the diverse cultural backgrounds of Asian Americans, non-Asian therapists must have an understanding of the cultural differences between themselves and their clients and be able to adapt their methods accordingly. This article identifies common errors made by non-Asian therapists and outlines appropriate therapeutic strategies.

Watts, A. W. (1961). *Psychotherapy East and West.* New York: Ballantine.

This book makes important connections between Western psychotherapy techniques and Eastern philosophies by identifying and comparing major focal points of Western psychotherapy and such Eastern philosophies as Buddhism, Vedanta, Yoga, and Taoism. This book leads readers to integrate for themselves aspects of both Western and Eastern approaches.

Waxer, P. H. (1989). Cantonese versus Canadian evaluation of directive and non-directive therapy. *Canadian Journal of Counseling*, *23*(3), 263–272.

An outline and presentation of the results of a study that support the contention that North American clientele view counseling as an "explorative and democratic process" while Asian clientele view counseling as "a more directive, paternalistic and autocratic process."

Wu, D. Y., & Tseng, W. (1985). The characteristics of Chinese culture. In W. Tseng & D. Y. Wu (Eds.). *Chinese culture and mental health*. Orlando, FL: Academic Press.

This article focuses on the various aspects of Chinese culture that have an impact on the state of mental health services for Chinese people.

Yamamoto, J., & Acosta, F. X. (1982). Treatment of Asian Americans and Hispanic Americans: Similarities and differences. *Journal of the American Academy of Psychoanalysis*, *10*(4), 585–607.

The authors discuss the various cultural and economic issues that affect therapy with Asian and Hispanic Americans. The article highlights the similarities and differences between the two subcultural groups.

Index

About the Authors and Contributors

JEAN LAU CHIN, Ed.D., is Executive Director of South Cove Community Health Center in Boston. She is a psychologist who has practiced for more than 20 years, providing psychotherapy, consultation, program development, community health/mental health administration, and training of mental health professionals. She co-directed a child guidance clinic and has given numerous presentations on psychotherapy and culture and on the practice and delivery of culturally competent services for Asian American populations.

MARYANNA DOMOKOS-CHENG HAM, Ed.D., is Associate Professor of Psychology at the University of Massachusetts–Boston. In her clinical practice and teaching, she has developed techniques for implementing the theoretical concept of empathy. Her research has examined relationships between individuals, among family members, and among ethnic and racial groups.

GEORGE K. HONG, Ph.D., is Associate Professor in the Division of Administration and Counseling, School of Education, at California State University–Los Angeles. He is also a clinical psychologist and has extensive experience in providing services to the Asian American community. He is active in research and development of multicultural mental health services.

JOAN HUSER LIEM, Ph.D., is Associate Professor of Psychology at the University of Massachusetts–Boston. Dr. Liem is a clinical psychologist whose research, teaching, and clinical practice focus on individual and family responses to a variety of stressful experiences: unemployment, separation and divorce, mental illness, and physical and sexual abuse. She is one of the founders of a new Ph.D. program in clinical psychology at the University of Massachusetts–Boston that emphasizes social and cultural perspectives on human development and clinical psychology, especially as they affect understanding of ethnic minority and low-income groups.

SIU PING MA, MSW, is at Richmond Area Maxi Center Services in San Francisco.

GLORIA CHIEKO SAITO, Ph.D. is a clinical psychologist at Counseling and Psychological Services at the University of California, Berkeley. She is also Director for Training for Berkeley's APA-accredited pre-doctoral internship program. She has worked extensively with Asian Americans in the Bay Area, including refugee and immigrant populations.

JENNIE H. Y. YEE, Ph.D., is a clinical psychologist at the Child Development Center, Chinatown/North Beach Clinical Services in San Francisco.